The *Americans with Disabilities Act:* What Supervisors Need to Know

The *Americans with Disabilities Act:* What Supervisors Need to Know

JOAN ACKERSTEIN, J.D.

The Business Skills Express Series

BUSINESS ONE IRWIN/MIRROR PRESS
Burr Ridge, Illinois
New York, New York
Boston, Massachusetts

This symbol indicates that the paper in this book is made of recycled paper. Its fiber content exceeds the recommended minimum of 50% waste paper fibers as specified by the EPA.

© RICHARD D. IRWIN, INC., 1994

All rights reserved. No part of this publication may be reproduced, stored in a retrieval system, or transmitted, in any form or by any means, electronic, mechanical, photocopying, recording, or otherwise, without the prior written permission of the publisher.

This publication is designed to provide accurate and authoritative information in regard to the subject matter covered. It is sold with the understanding that neither the author nor the publisher is engaged in rendering legal, accounting, or other professional service. If legal advice or other expert assistance is required, the services of a competent professional person should be sought.

From a Declaration of Principles jointly adopted by a Committee of the American Bar Association and a Committee of Publishers.

Mirror Press:	David R. Helmstadter
	Carla F. Tishler
Editor-in-chief:	Jeffrey A. Krames
Project editor:	Stephanie M. Britt
Production manager:	Diane Palmer
Designer:	Jeanne M. Rivera
Art coordinator:	Heather Burbridge
Illustrator:	Boston Graphics, Inc.
Compositor:	Alexander Graphics
Typeface:	12/14 Criterion
Printer:	Malloy Lithographing, Inc.

Library of Congress Cataloging-in-Publication Data

Ackerstein, Joan.
    The Americans with Disabilities Act, what supervisors need to know / Joan Ackerstein.
       p.   cm.—(The Business skills express series)
    ISBN 1-55623-889-4
    1. Handicapped—Employment—United States.   2. Handicapped—Employment—Law and legislation—United States.   I. Title.
II. Series.
HD7256.U5A65   1994
658.3'045—dc20

93–10689

Printed in the United States of America
1 2 3 4 5 6 7 8 9 0 ML 0 9 8 7 6 5 4 3

PREFACE

The Americans with Disabilities Act (ADA) of 1990 was the culmination of a lengthy effort to obtain broad protection for disabled persons. There were statutes in effect that provided some protection: the Rehabilitation Act of 1973 protected disabled persons employed by enterprises that received federal funds, and over 40 states had statutes that provided some protection to the disabled. Never before, however, had there been a comprehensive plan to protect disabled persons from discrimination in employment and in other contexts.

In passing the legislation, Congress recognized that it was spending more than $60 billion annually on programs for the 43 million disabled Americans. It also recognized that while two thirds of disabled persons between the ages of 16 and 64 wanted to work, that same two thirds was unemployed. The ADA was an effort to remedy this problem.

Title I of the ADA, the Title prohibiting discrimination in employment, became effective on July 26, 1992, for employers with 25 or more employees. It becomes effective on July 26, 1994, for employers with 15 or more employees. The impact of Title I was felt immediately. In the first five months after enactment, the Equal Employment Opportunity Commission, which administers the act, received approximately 3,358 charges of discrimination. These included claims for wrongful discharge (46.1 percent), for noncompliance with the "reasonable accommodation provision" (20.4 percent), for hiring discrimination (15.4 percent), for harassment (9 percent), for denial of benefits (3.4 percent), and for discrimination in other terms and conditions of employment (23.4 percent). Specific impairments alleged included back conditions (14.7 percent), mental illness (7.9 percent), diabetes (3.8 percent), heart conditions (3.6 percent), alcoholism (2.3 percent), and AIDS (1.8 percent).

There are four other ADA titles. Title II of the ADA prohibits discrimination by a public entity, including any state or local government. Title III, applicable to public accommodations and commercial facilities such as hotels and theaters, requires that facilities and services be accessible to individuals with disabilities. Title IV is applicable to common carriers engaged in interstate or intrastate communication and is intended to ensure that persons with speech and hearing disabilities have the same level of accessibility as people who do not have these disabilities. Title V includes miscellaneous ADA provisions.

The requirements imposed on employers by Title I can be stated briefly. The ADA prohibits employers from discriminating against qualified applicants or employees who can perform the essential functions of a job with or without reasonable accommodation. Once you understand the terms used by the ADA, such as *essential functions, reasonable accommodation, prohibited discrimination,* and *undue hardship,* the statute becomes comprehensible.

This book covers Title I of the ADA and is designed to assist the supervisor, manager, or human resources professional in understanding and applying the ADA. Each chapter defines a significant ADA principle and includes specific examples showing how the principle is applied. This unique feature will enhance your understanding of the ADA because it applies the statute's provisions to the kinds of ADA issues that arise routinely in your workplace. Each chapter also includes exercises and Chapter Checkpoints that enable you to measure your understanding as you progress through the chapters. A handy glossary provides quick definitions of key ADA terms. The full text of Title I of the ADA appears in a separate appendix for easy reference. ADA regulations are not reprinted in their entirety but are excerpted throughout the book.

Joan Ackerstein

About the Author

Joan Ackerstein is a partner in the national law firm of Jackson, Lewis, Schnitzer & Krupman, which represents management in labor, employment, and benefits law matters. She specializes in state and federal civil rights law, providing protection from discrimination and sexual harassment, and in matters involving wrongful termination. She counsels employers on related workplace issues. Ms. Ackerstein is a former Assistant United States Attorney for the District of Massachusetts, Civil Division. A member of the Massachusetts and New York bar associations, she is a frequent speaker and author on labor and employment issues. Ms. Ackerstein's law degree is from the Georgetown University Law Center.

About Business One Irwin

Business One Irwin is the nation's premier publisher of business books. As a Times Mirror company, we work closely with Times Mirror training organizations, including Zenger-Miller, Inc., Learning International, Inc., and Kaset International, to serve the training needs of business and industry.

About the Business Skills Express Series

This expanding series of authoritative, concise, and fast-paced books delivers high quality training on key business topics at a remarkably affordable cost. The series will help managers, supervisors, and front line personnel in organizations of all sizes and types hone their business skills while enhancing job performance and career satisfaction.

Business Skills Express books are ideal for employee seminars, independent self-study, on-the-job training, and classroom-based instruction. Express books are also convenient-to-use references at work.

CONTENTS

Self-Assessment   xv

Chapter 1   1
Identifying a Disability
Disability Quiz   1
What Is a Disability?   2

Chapter 2   9
Prohibited Discrimination
Definition of Discrimination   10
Performance Standards   14

Chapter 3   19
Essential Functions
Identifying Essential Functions   20

Chapter 4   27
Reasonable Accommodation
Types of Accommodation   28
When Reasonable Accommodation Is Necessary under the ADA   29
How to Determine a Reasonable Accommodation   31
What an Employer Must Do to Reasonably Accommodate   32

Chapter 5
Undue Hardship — 37
How to Determine Undue Hardship 38

Chapter 6
Preemployment Inquiries — 43
Prohibited Inquiries 43
Permissible Inquiries 44
Permissible Inquiries for Obviously Disabled Applicants 45

Chapter 7
Medical Examinations — 49
Preemployment Medical Examinations 49
Withdrawing a Job Offer 52
Conducting the Preemployment Examination 53
Postemployment Medical Examinations 53

Chapter 8
Qualification Standards and Selection Criteria — 57
Qualification Standards 57
Selection Criteria 60

Chapter 9
Drugs and Alcohol — 63
Exclusion for Illegal Drug Use 63
Actions the Employer May Take 65

Chapter 10
Filing Charges and Available Remedies 69
   Filing the ADA Charge 70
   Processing the Charge of Discrimination 71
   Proving Discrimination in a Lawsuit 72
   Recoverable Damages 73

Postscript 78

Post-Test 79

Title I of the Americans with Disabilities Act of 1990 83

Suggested Solutions 93

Glossary 101

Self-Assessment

How do you feel about your understanding of the Americans with Disabilities Act? This simple self-assessment may confirm your confidence or may suggest areas for further study. In either case, it will provide a starting point for you as you begin your quest for a greater understanding of the ADA.

	Almost Always	Sometimes	Almost Never
1. I am confident that I know the conditions that constitute disabilities under the ADA.	_____	_____	_____
2. I know when there is an obligation to accommodate a disabled employee.	_____	_____	_____
3. I am sure of my ability to write job descriptions that are suitable under the ADA.	_____	_____	_____
4. I know the questions I can ask when I interview job applicants.	_____	_____	_____
5. I understand the ADA's restrictions on preemployment medical examinations.	_____	_____	_____
6. I have no difficulty handling incidents involving employees' drug or alcohol abuse.	_____	_____	_____
7. I know when an accommodation is unnecessary because it would constitute an undue hardship.	_____	_____	_____
8. Our workplace social activities conform to the ADA.	_____	_____	_____
9. Our employment recruiters comply with the ADA.	_____	_____	_____
10. I understand when we can discipline a disabled employee.	_____	_____	_____
11. I know what actions constitute discrimination under the ADA.	_____	_____	_____
12. I know how an employee brings an action for ADA discrimination.	_____	_____	_____

The *Americans with Disabilities Act:* What Supervisors Need to Know

CHAPTER

1 | Identifying a Disability

This chapter will help you to:

- Recognize the circumstances that identify an applicant or employee as disabled under the ADA.

Mary Rodriguez is an excellent recruiter for her employer, a supermarket chain. She always manages to identify the applicant's strengths and weaknesses. She decided not to hire Gary Peterson, a qualified applicant with a history of back trouble, for a position as a stock clerk. Mary was concerned that Gary might reinjure his back while hauling cases of groceries from the storage room. If he reinjured his back, the store would be left shorthanded. Gary filed a charge of discrimination, claiming he was refused employment due to his disability. ∎

Does Gary have a valid claim under the ADA? If so, what did Mary do wrong? _____

DISABILITY QUIZ

How do you define the term *disabled?* List some characteristics that you would consider disabling. _____

Ask yourself the following questions:

- Does a condition have to be life-threatening to be disabling?
- What if the disabling condition is temporary?

Would these people qualify as disabled?

- What if the person makes a full recovery?
- What if the person's own actions contributed to the condition?
- What if the condition only affects the person's mental state?

WHAT IS A DISABILITY?

The ADA provides that a person is considered to have a disability in three circumstances. Section 3(2) of the ADA defines disability as

(A) a physical or mental impairment that substantially limits one or more major life activities of such individual;

(B) a record of such an impairment; or

(C) being regarded as having such an impairment.

These categories sound easy to identify, but what actually is included in these categories? Do the categories include a person who uses drugs? How about alcohol? Do they include dyslexia? How about a physical deformity?

Physical or Mental Impairment

The first classification of a disability is the most common. An individual has a disability if he or she has a physical or mental disorder that substantially limits his or her ability to perform or take part in major life activities. These life activities include, for example, walking, seeing, hearing, speaking, working, and learning. While not specifically defined by the ADA, physical or mental impairments that substantially limit major life activities include:

- Cancer.
- Organic brain syndrome.
- Heart disease.
- Certain learning disabilities.
- Diabetes.
- Emotional or mental illness.
- Cosmetic disfigurement.
- Hearing loss.
- Anatomical loss.
- Arthritis.
- Speech disorders.
- HIV infection.

Since the physical or mental disorder must substantially limit major life activities, temporary disabilities—a broken arm that heals normally or a normal pregnancy—will not be considered disabilities.

The ADA identifies certain conditions that do not constitute physical or mental impairments. These include:

- Physical characteristics such as eye color, hair color, or left-handedness.
- A predisposition to illness or disease.
- Normal pregnancy.

- Poor judgment.
- Quick temper.
- Environmental or cultural disadvantages (lack of education or prison record).
- Temporary impairments with little or no long-term impact.
- Concussions.
- Current illegal use of drugs.
- Homosexuality or bisexuality.
- Compulsive gambling.
- Pyromania.
- Kleptomania.

Exercise 1.1

Check those employees who have a disabling condition under the ADA. Explanatory answers are at the end of the book.

☐ 1. Sally Lowenstein is a secretary in underwriting who was out of work for four weeks with a broken ankle. Her manager must decide if she has a disability because Sally is asking to have her desk moved closer to the elevator so she does not have to walk so far at work.

☐ 2. Tom Rodriguez is a shipping clerk who just went on workers' compensation with a herniated disc. His manager wants to replace him because he may be recuperating for several months.

☐ 3. Mary Henderson works in accounting. She is a diabetic who controls her disease with diet and exercise. She is asking to work only four days a week due to this condition.

☐ 4. Harry Fairweather is a nurse who is a homosexual. He wants to work only the day shift because he says the evening shift harasses him about his lifestyle.

☐ 5. John Washington is a systems analyst in perfect health but has a large scar on his face due to a childhood injury. He claims that he has not been promoted to a managerial position because he would have contact with more people and his scar is unsightly.

Record of Impairment

Persons having a record of impairment are those who had a recognized disability in the past. They are included as disabled under the ADA to ensure that they are not discriminated against as a result of their past history. This category would include:

- An applicant who has been out of work for a year while she recovered from a heart attack.
- An employee who spent six months in a psychiatric hospital.
- A recovering alcoholic.
- An employee treated for bleeding ulcers five years ago.

Exercise 1.2

Check those employees who have a record of impairment under the ADA. Explanations appear at the end of the book.

☐ 1. Lena Rose is a salesperson who is fully recovered from cancer. Her manager does not allow her to work overtime because she fears Lena is not strong enough.

☐ 2. Nina Tirendi is a systems analyst who recovered from a broken arm she had a year ago. She claims that she received less of a bonus than the other people in the department because she was out for six weeks.

☐ 3. Michael Russo was hospitalized two years ago for drug addiction and he has not used drugs since. His employer refuses to let him meet with customers, a function performed by all other employees in the store.

☐ 4. Charles Fernald is in good health but last year, after he turned 50, he lost most of his hair and was almost bald within six months. He claims that he was not promoted because he now looks too old.

Regarded as Having an Impairment

Persons regarded as having an impairment are those who do not have a disability but are protected under the ADA because they are perceived as having a disability. This category includes the following situations:

- The employer perceives the employee to have an impairment even though it is not substantially limiting.
- The employee has an impairment that is substantially limiting only because of the attitudes of others toward the impairment.
- The employee has no impairment but is regarded as having one.

Examples of people regarded as having an impairment would include:

- An employee with mild hypertension.
- A cosmetics salesperson with a small facial scar.
- A waiter rumored to have AIDS.

Exercise 1.3

Check those persons who would be regarded as having an impairment under the ADA. Explanations appear at the end of the book.

☐ 1. Ron Shem-Tov is gay. His co-workers believe that he is HIV positive.

☐ 2. Martha Healy is applying for employment. She is pregnant.

☐ 3. Rene Sontag's employer will not let him work overtime because Rene had a mild heart attack five years ago. The employer fears that Rene will have another one.

☐ 4. Lisa Jacobson works in the accounting department with 15 other employees who all feel that she is difficult to work with because she has a quick temper.

Chapter Checkpoints

✓ An employee or applicant for employment will be considered disabled under the ADA if he or she:

   Has a physical or mental impairment.

   Has a record of impairment.

   Is regarded as having an impairment.

✓ If a person is not disabled within the meaning of the ADA, the protections of the ADA are not applicable.

✓ If a person is disabled within the meaning of the ADA, his or her employer or prospective employer may not discriminate against him or her due to that disability.

CHAPTER 2
Prohibited Discrimination

This chapter will help you to:
- Identify the actions that constitute prohibited discrimination under the ADA.

Jim Springer uses a wheelchair because of paralysis resulting from an accident some years ago. He was offered a job by Atlas Electronics and is doing very well. Six months after he began employment, Atlas scheduled a holiday party at a restaurant that is not wheelchair accessible. Jim complained to Lee Otis, Atlas's human resources manager. Lee said the plans were made and there was nothing he could do. Lee was not worried about the ADA because Atlas hired Jim and was paying him well. ■

Was Lee right not to worry about the ADA? Why or why not?
_____
_____

It is unlawful under the ADA to discriminate against a qualified invidividual with a disability by considering that disability when acting with regard to the individual's employment. Specifically, Section 102(a) of the ADA provides that

> No covered entity shall discriminate against a qualified individual with a disability because of the disability of such individual in regard to job application procedures, the hiring, advancement, or discharge of employees, employee compensation, job training, and other terms, conditions, and privileges of employment.

In other words, employers may not consider a disability when deciding on issues such as:

- Recruitment and advertising.
- Hiring, promotion, transfer, termination, layoff, or right of return from layoff.
- Rates of pay, compensation, and changes in compensation.
- Job assignments.
- Leaves of absence and sick leave.
- Fringe benefits.
- Selection and financial support for training and conferences.
- Social and recreational activities sponsored by the employer.
- Any other term, condition, or privilege of employment.

In addition to requiring that employers refrain from discriminating against an applicant or employee with a disability in the terms and conditions of employment, the ADA has another prohibition against discrimination. Section 503(a) of the ADA provides that

> No person shall discriminate against any individual because such individual has opposed any act or practice made unlawful by this Act or because such individual made a charge, testified, assisted or participated in any manner in an investigation, proceeding or hearing under this Act.

DEFINITION OF DISCRIMINATION

Section 102(b) of the ADA lists seven categories of actions that will be included within the term *discriminate* under the ADA. Examples follow each category.

1. **Limiting, segregating, or classifying an applicant or employee in a way that adversely affects him or her because of a disability**

An employer may not prohibit an employee with a heart condition from working overtime for fear that his or her condition will worsen. An employer may not deny a sales position to an applicant with the use of only one arm for fear that customers will be disturbed by that condition.

2. **Participating in a contractual or other relationship that has the effect of discriminating against an applicant or employee**

An employer may not use a recruiting agency that asks applicants if they have any disabilities or if they have ever received any psychiatric treatment.

An employer may not hold a training meeting at a conference center that is not accessible to disabled employees.

3. Using standards that have the effect of discriminating on the basis of disability or perpetuating the discrimination of others

An employer may have to modify policies that, though they appear neutral, have a disparate impact on disabled persons. Policies that may have a disparate impact include policies such as "every employee must have a driver's license" or "every employee must work 40 hours per week." Such policies are unlawful when they do not serve legitimate job-related functions. For example, a secretarial position with only word processing responsibilities does not require its occupant to know how to drive an automobile.

4. Denying jobs or benefits to an individual who has a relationship or an association with a disabled person (see the following section for more detail)

An employer may not exclude an employee from coverage under its medical plan because it knows that the employee has a seriously ill child whose medical expenses are very substantial. An employer may not deny a job to a qualified applicant because the applicant cares for a seriously ill parent.

5. Not making reasonable accommodation, unless the employer would suffer undue hardship.

An employer may not refuse an employee's request for leave to enter an alcohol treatment center, unless to do so would create an undue hardship on the operation of the business. An employer may not deny an employee's request that it buy an antiglare computer screen to reduce the glare that is a problem for his eye disorder when the cost to do so is only $39.

6. Using employment tests or selection criteria that tend to screen out disabled persons, unless the tests can be shown to be job related for the position in question and consistent with a business necessity.

An employer may give a typing test to applicants for secretarial positions even though those tests may screen out visually impaired persons. An employer may not ask applicants for a position as a stock clerk in a warehouse to perform 20 push-ups.

7. Failing to administer tests in a manner that assures that, when administered to disabled persons, the tests accurately reflect the person's skills.

An employer who gives applicants for a machine shop position a written test may have to give it orally to an applicant with dyslexia. An employer who tests applicants for a janitorial position may have to allow additional time for an employee who is mentally retarded.

Discrimination Based on the Applicant's or Employee's Relationship or Association with a Disabled Person

The ADA prohibits discrimination against an applicant or employee because of his or her relationship or association with a disabled person. Section 102(b)(4) provides that the term *discriminate* under the ADA will include

excluding or otherwise denying equal jobs or benefits to a qualified individual because of the known disability of an individual with whom the qualified individual is known to have a relationship or association.

In addition, section 1630.8 of the ADA regulations* provides that

> it is unlawful for a covered entity to exclude or deny equal jobs or benefits to, or otherwise discriminate against, a qualified individual because of the known disability of an individual with whom the qualified individual is known to have a family, business, social or other relationship or association.

The prohibition is designed to prevent employers from refusing to hire a person because of concern that he or she will be absent frequently to care for an ill family member or that the health insurance premiums will increase due to the family member's medical costs. Keep the following in mind:

- The ADA regulations do not define *family relationship*. Nonetheless, a spouse, child, or parent certainly would be included.
- The ADA does not define *relationship or association*. At a minimum, this phrase includes persons with whom the applicant or employee cohabitates or socializes.

Jean Gordon applies for a promotion to a position as an account executive with an advertising agency. The vice president who makes that decision is reluctant to promote Jean because he knows that her father is seriously ill and fears that she will be distracted or absent during a protracted illness. The denial of a promotion on that basis is a violation of the ADA. ∎

Bruce Kelly applies for a promotion to the position as food and beverage manager of a resort hotel. The general manager of the hotel knows that Bruce is a homosexual and that the partner with whom he lives has AIDS. The denial of a promotion on that basis is a violation of the ADA. ∎

The ADA does *not* require that an employer reasonably accommodate an applicant or employee who has a relationship with a disabled person. The reasonable accommodation requirement of the ADA is limited to persons who are in fact disabled.

---

*For the full text of regulations pertaining to the ADA, refer to the Code of Federal Regulations pertaining to PL 101-336 (Americans with Disabilities Act of 1990), available at most large public libraries or law libraries.

David Gutierrez is a graphics artist with a publishing firm who works full-time. He requests a part-time work schedule so that he is able to care for a seriously ill parent. The ADA does not require the employer to grant that request. However, a family or medical leave statute might. ■

PERFORMANCE STANDARDS

An employer can require that disabled employees meet the same standards of performance applicable to all other employees. However, an employee should not be downgraded because an accommodation is needed to perform a function of his or her position.

Karen Norris is a secretary for an engineering firm. Because of physical therapy she has three mornings a week, Karen starts work on those mornings at 9:30 A.M. instead of at 9:00 A.M. Karen's supervisor may not decrease her performance rating because she starts work later than the other secretaries. ■

An employer may also have an obligation to provide an employee with an accommodation during the evaluation process so that he or she can participate fully in the evaluation.

Richard Benoit is a hearing-impaired architect who is having performance difficulties. His supervisor wants to have a meeting with Richard to discuss these difficulties and to set goals for his performance improvement. The supervisor may be required to provide a sign language interpreter for the meeting so that Richard can understand fully the supervisor's expectations. ■

An employer may not reduce an employee's compensation because it modified his or her job duties by removing marginal functions to accommodate a disability.

Greg Johnson is one of a number of employees in the mailroom of the corporate headquarters of a manufacturing firm. Because Greg injured his back last year, he no longer delivers heavy packages throughout the firm. His duties are limited to sorting the mail and pushing the mail cart. Other mailroom employees now deliver the packages. The firm may not reduce Greg's wages since the function he no longer performs is only a marginal function of his job. ∎

If an employee is reassigned to a different job because of a disability or takes a part-time position, the employer may modify compensation.

William Hogan was a full-time social worker. After beginning treatment for cancer, William found that he could work only half-days because of fatigue. His employer was willing to create a part-time position for William. The employer could reduce William's salary to reflect his part-time hours without violating the ADA. ∎

Remember: The ADA does not require that employers give a preference to disabled applicants or employees. It only requires that the employer refrain from discrimination due to a disability.

Laura Matthews and Rob Kramer both applied for a promotion to the chief auditor position. They have almost identical experience and performance ratings. Sam Bacon, the department manager, knows that Rob has diabetes. Sam does not have to give Rob a preference due to Rob's disability. Sam does not violate the ADA by promoting Laura because he feels that she has developed better relationships with her co-workers. ∎

Exercise 2.1

Check those situations that may involve the employer engaging in an act of prohibited discrimination under the ADA. Explanatory answers are at the end of the book.

☐ 1. XYZ Manufacturing is opening a new plant and will be hiring 300 new employees. An employment agency is being used for its recruiting. Alan Packman, the human resources manager, tells the agency to look for healthy applicants in order to keep insurance costs down.

☐ 2. Angela Diaz was accounting supervisor for three years. She was doing a great job. The position of accounting manager became available. Angela was being actively considered. Then Angela's mother had a stroke and Angela was going to need some time off. Angela's name was removed from consideration for the position.

☐ 3. Industries, Inc., was offering a computer training course to its supervisors. It would pay for the program, a course given at a local college that met four hours a week for 16 weeks. Henry Goldmen, age 64, wanted to attend. Laura Bell, the human resources manager, reviewed his application. Laura knew that Henry had been treated last year for colon cancer. Laura felt badly that she had decided to deny Henry's application. He might not be able to work long enough to make the training worthwhile.

☐ 4. John Irvine had been sick all winter and finally, in March, told his supervisor that he had AIDS. After John missed six weeks of work, his manager made a decision to terminate him. The manager just could not continue to keep the position open.

☐ 5. Alice Monroe applied for a position as a salesperson in an upscale department store. However, Alice had a noticeable facial disfigurement. The hiring manager decided not to hire Alice despite her experience because of a concern that customers would not make purchases from her.

Exercise 2.2

Some people are most sympathetic to those with disabilities. If you ask, they say that they go out of their way to help those with disabilities. These people never discriminate. Or do they? Consider the examples below, and answer the questions that follow. Explanatory answers are at the end of the book.

1. Carol Ann Leonard is marketing director of a computer software company. Ray Pierson is a sales representative whose performance has been marginal since he lost a limb six months ago. Carol knows she should sit down with Ray and give him some constructive criticism. However, she does not want to put more pressure on him. How can Carol Ann handle Ray's performance problem? _____
_____
_____
_____
_____

2. Joe Belonni is a production manager at a manufacturing plant. Because of an unexpected surge in orders, Joe needs some of his employees to work overtime. He decides not to ask Michael

Ashland. He knows that Michael's back has been bothering him. Joe decides it might be too much for Michael. Should Joe have offered Michael overtime? Why or why not? _____

_____

_____

_____

_____

3. Kevin O'Toole, a human resources manager, knew that Larry Blye was having difficulty in his engineering position. Kevin thought that it might be because of Larry's hearing impairment. He decided to transfer Kevin to a different department which had another hearing-impaired employee. Kevin thought that it might be easier for Larry to work with another hearing-impaired employee. Can Kevin transfer Larry to another department to be with another disabled employee? Why or why not? _____

_____

_____

_____

_____

Chapter Checkpoints

✓ The ADA prohibits employers from discriminating against disabled applicants or employees when acting with regard to their employment.

✓ The ADA prohibits employers from denying employment opportunities or benefits to an individual who has an association with a disabled person.

✓ An employer may require that disabled employees meet standards of performance applicable to employees without disabilities.

✓ An employer may not retaliate against any applicant or employee who opposes an act or practice that violates the ADA.

CHAPTER 3
Essential Functions

This chapter will help you to:
- Identify the essential functions of a job within the meaning of the ADA.

Tom Williams applied for a job as a research assistant at a large biotechnology company. Tom had an excellent interview. As he was leaving the interview, Ann Chung, the human resources manager, noticed that Tom had a severe limp. Suspecting that Tom would have a problem with the amount of walking the job sometimes required, such as moving between various laboratories at the company, Ann did not offer him the position. Tom filed a discrimination charge against the company, claiming that he was not hired because of his disability. Nowhere in the job description did it say that walking between labs, or even working in more than one lab, was an essential or even marginal function of the job. ∎

Does Tom have a valid claim under the ADA? If so, what did Ann do wrong?

The ADA precludes an employer from discriminating against a qualified individual with a disability who can perform the essential functions of the job with or without reasonable accommodation. Specifically, Section 101(8) of the ADA defines a qualified individual with a disability as

an individual with a disability who, with or without reasonable accommodation, can perform the essential functions of the employment position that such individual holds or desires. For the purposes of this title, consideration shall be given to the employer's judgment as to what functions of a job are essential, and if an employer has prepared a written description before advertising or interviewing applicants for the job, this description shall be considered evidence of the essential functions of the job.

Complying with the ADA requires the following two-step approach. The employer should consider the second step only if he or she finds that the individual is otherwise qualified.

1. Determine whether the individual is otherwise qualified. That is, does the person satisfy the education, skills, and experience prerequisites of the job? For example,

    Does the candidate for a nursing position hold the necessary nursing degree and state license?

    Does a candidate for a word processing position have the two years of experience required?

    Does a candidate for an accounting position have the requisite B.S. in accounting?

2. Determine whether the person can perform the essential functions of the job, with or without reasonable accommodation.

The ADA requires that a person's ability to do a job be measured by analyzing the *essential* functions of the job. The ADA distinguishes between essential and marginal functions and prohibits employers from refusing to hire or promote based on a person's inability to perform a marginal function of a job. These examples illustrate the distinction.

A commercial airline pilot loses her sight in an accident. There is no accommodation that will enable her to perform an essential function of her job, flying a plane. Removal from the position for that reason does not violate the ADA.

A commercial airline pilot is unable to stand for long periods of time and can no longer wish passengers good-bye as they depart. This function is clearly marginal, and a discharge based on her inability to perform it would violate the ADA.

IDENTIFYING ESSENTIAL FUNCTIONS

The ADA requires an employer to consider only the essential functions of a job in determining whether a person with a disability is qualified. Therefore, the employer must identify those functions of a job that are essential as opposed to marginal.

Essential Functions

Employees must identify essential job functions.

Regulations of the Equal Employment Opportunity Commission (EEOC) provide that a job function may be essential for one of the following reasons (examples follow):

1. The position exists to perform that function.

A nurse is hired to care for patients. Caring for patients is an essential function of the job because removing that function would fundamentally alter the job.

2. There are only a limited number of employees available to perform the function.

A night security guard for a manufacturing plant is required to answer the telephone. That function is essential because there are no other employees available to answer the calls.

3. The function is so specialized that the incumbent is hired for his or her expertise or ability to perform that function.

An art teacher is hired for her knowledge of art history and her talent as a painter. Painting is an essential function because the art teacher is hired for that specific ability.

Factors Reviewed in Essential Function Analysis

There are particular factors that will be examined by the EEOC to determine if a function is essential. These include:

- The employer's judgment as to what functions are essential.
- Information included in the job description if it was prepared before the advertising or interviewing began.
- The amount of time spent performing the function.
- The consequences of not requiring the employee to perform the function.
- The terms of an applicable collective bargaining agreement.
- The work experience of current and past employees in the job.

Job Descriptions

Job descriptions are helpful in identifying the essential functions of a job. They also help to do the following (examples follow):

1. Identify the interview questions used for applicants.

The job description for an office manager requires the individual to supervise 10 to 15 secretaries and purchase supplies, computer equipment, and office furniture. Because these functions are outlined in the job description, the human resources manager knows to ask applicants about their supervisory experience and knowledge of buying supplies and furniture.

2. Permit a physician to assist in the determination of whether a person can perform the essential functions of a job.

A position description lists the weight of a medication cart a nurse will be required to maneuver. As a result, the physician examining an applicant with a back condition will be able to determine if the applicant can accomplish that task.

Some tips for developing job descriptions include:

- Analyze each position carefully.
- Talk to people currently holding the job and their supervisors to find out what they do.

- If possible, observe the workers under a range of conditions.
- Decide which functions of the job are essential and which are marginal.
- Review production records to ensure that production standards set out in the job description reflect actual work performed.
- Make sure that the job description is accurate.
- Inquire as to the amount of time spent on various tasks.
- Exclude vague entries on the job description such as other miscellaneous duties.
- Review job descriptions regularly to ensure that they reflect changes in positions that are made from time to time.

Exercise 3.1

Check those functions that you would consider essential to the positions with which they are matched. Explanatory answers are at the end of the book.

☐ 1. *Accounting clerk:* carrying file boxes up from the basement during the two weeks before company tax returns are due.

☐ 2. *Ward nurse:* being able to lift an unconscious adult off the floor.

☐ 3. *Medical equipment salesperson:* being able to deliver medical equipment to the buyer.

☐ 4. *Short-order cook:* being able to prepare meals for patrons at a 30-seat cafeteria.

☐ 5. *Claims adjuster:* being able to type 60 words per minute.

Exercise 3.2

Complete parts A and B below.

Part A: How do you determine the essential functions of a job? Take a few minutes to prepare a list of the essential functions for a secretarial position in your department. For example:

- Is typing an essential function?
- Is running errands from time to time an essential function?
- Is being available to work from 9:00 A.M. to 5:00 P.M. Monday through Friday an essential function?

- If the secretary only files once a week for two hours, is that an essential function?
- If the secretary takes telephone messages but there is also a receptionist who can do it, is taking messages an essential function?
- Is being able to draft letters an essential function?
- If the secretary prepares expense reports once a month, is that an essential function?
- Is the ability to be available for overtime an essential function?

Part B: Fill out the job description started below for a secretarial position in your department. A sample solution appears at the end of the book.

Job title: Secretary
Department: Human Resources
General summary: Under the general direction of the office administrator; completes secretarial and clerical work for the Human Resources Department

---

Essential Functions and Responsibilities:

_____
_____
_____
_____
_____

Marginal Functions:

_____
_____
_____
_____
_____

Knowledge, Ability, and Other Job Requirements:

_____
_____
_____
_____
_____

Chapter Checkpoints

✓ Although the ADA prohibits an employer from discriminating against qualified individuals with disabilities, an employer does not have to hire, promote, or retain anyone who is not qualified to perform the essential functions of the job with or without reasonable accommodation.

✓ Employers should determine the essential functions of each position and distinguish these essential functions from marginal functions.

✓ As a preventative measure, all essential functions should be contained in the job description for each position. These descriptions should be developed and revised regularly.

✓ To avoid challenges to what it deems essential functions, an employer should be careful to develop accurate job descriptions. If a job description is accurately prepared before advertising or interviewing applicants, it will be evidence of a job's essential functions.

✓ An individual's ability to perform the essential functions of a job must be decided at the time of the hiring, promotion, transfer, or other employment decision at issue. It may not be determined by speculating as to an applicant's or employee's future capabilities.

✓ Once you have developed an appropriate job description, it is advisable to use it in job notices and in the advertising and recruiting effort.

CHAPTER 4
Reasonable Accommodation

This chapter will help you to:
- Identify the employer's obligation under the ADA to reasonably accommodate qualified applicants for employment or employees.

Margaret Grady is a receptionist for an advertising agency. Her duties consist of answering the telephone, scheduling conference rooms, ensuring the availability of coffee at meetings, and arranging for taxis and lunches. Every midmorning, she also walks to the basement mailroom in an adjoining building and picks up the agency's mail.

Two months ago, Margaret had a heart attack. While she now is back to work, her physician advised her against walking up and down stairs. Margaret asked Elaine Samson, the agency administrator, if someone else could pick up the daily mail, a task that takes about half an hour. Elaine said they would try, but if they could not find another employee available to do the task, they would have to ask Margaret to leave the agency since she could no longer perform all of her duties. ∎

Is Elaine right? Why or why not? _____

Under the ADA, employers must provide a qualified applicant or employee with a reasonable accommodation if a disability prevents the individual from performing the essential functions of a job *and* there is a reasonable accommodation that permits them to do the essential functions of the job. An accommodation under the ADA is a change in the work environment that enables a qualified applicant or employee with a disability to participate in all of the benefits of the workplace.

Specifically, Section 102(b)(5)(A) of the ADA provides that an employer may be deemed to be discriminating under the ADA if it does not make "reasonable accommodations to the known physical or mental limitations of an otherwise qualified individual with a disability who is an applicant or employee. . . ." Section 101(9) of the ADA provides that reasonable accommodation may include:

(A) making existing facilities used by employees readily accessible to and usable by individuals with disabilities; and

(B) job restructuring, part-time or modified work schedules, reassignment to a vacant position, acquisition or modification of equipment or devices, appropriate adjustment or modifications of examinations, training materials or policies, the provision of qualified readers or interpreters, and other similar accommodations for individuals with disabilities.

TYPES OF ACCOMMODATION

The ADA identifies three types of accommodation. (Examples follow.)

1. Accommodations that ensure equal opportunity in the application process.

A person with a visual disability may need assistance in filling out an application for employment.

2. Accommodations that enable employees to perform the essential functions of the job.

An employee with a hearing impairment may need a telephone amplifier to enable her to use a telephone to call customers.

3. Accommodations that enable employees to enjoy equal benefits of employment.

An employer should ensure that a holiday party held off premises is accessible by an employee who uses a wheelchair.

The ADA recognizes that qualified applicants or employees face a variety of barriers to employment. These include:

- Physical barriers that make it difficult to get to or around the work site.

Some reasonable accommodations are straightforward; others may be less tangible.

- Communication barriers.
- Rigid work schedules that do not permit flexibility for taking a medical leave or receiving medical treatment.
- Barriers that are created by people's perceptions, such as unfounded fears, stereotypes, and misconceptions about safety and absenteeism.

WHEN REASONABLE ACCOMMODATION IS NECESSARY UNDER THE ADA

To decide whether a reasonable accommodation is necessary, the employer must first answer some preliminary questions:

1. Does the applicant or employee have a disability, as opposed to a temporary condition or condition such as illegal drug use which is not considered a disability under the ADA?
2. Is the applicant or employee otherwise qualified?
3. Can the applicant or employee perform the essential functions of the job?

If the employer determines that it should consider a reasonable accommodation because the applicant or employee has a disability and is otherwise qualified, it should keep these principles in mind:

- Most frequently, though not always, it is the obligation of an individual with a disability to request a reasonable accommodation.
- If the cost of an accommodation would impose an undue hardship on the employer, the individual with a disability should be given the option of providing the accommodation or paying a portion of its cost.
- A reasonable accommodation need not be the best accommodation as long as it is effective.
- The reasonable accommodation obligation applies only to accommodations that reduce barriers to employment—it does not require an employer to provide a disabled person with an accommodation that the person requests for another reason.
- If an individual requests an accommodation and the need for the accommodation is not obvious, or the employer does not believe it is needed, the employer may request documentation of the individual's limitations to support the request.

How the Need to Reasonably Accommodate Arises

The ADA requires employers to provide reasonable accommodations to otherwise qualified applicants or employees with disabilities. How does that need arise? Sometimes it will begin with a request of the disabled applicant or employee for accommodation, as with the request of Margaret Grady, in the case cited above. In what other ways do you think that need may arise?

What if the employee does not request an accommodation? May the employer still have an obligation to reasonably accommodate even if the employee does not make a request?

Since his hospitalization last month, Larry Hines's performance decreases significantly during the last two hours of his shift. Should his foreman ask him if he would like to work fewer hours per day rather than disciplining him for poor performance? The answer is yes. ■

What is the impact of poor performance? Might an employer be charged with knowing from an employee's performance difficulties that some accommodation is necessary?

Wendy Rose's supervisor suspects that Wendy has an alcohol problem that has caused the dramatic decline in her performance. Should the supervisor consider an accommodation prior to discharge? The answer is yes. ■

What if a supervisor has knowledge of a disability? Might that knowledge be sufficient to require the employer to reasonably accommodate?

Gwen Mesidor is in a wheelchair. Her employer will be holding a two-day training conference off-site. Gwen's department will be invited. Does the employer have an obligation to ensure that the site is wheelchair accessible? Again, the answer is yes. ■

HOW TO DETERMINE A REASONABLE ACCOMMODATION

Once the employer determines that a reasonable accommodation is appropriate, how does the employer decide what the accommodation should be?

The ADA contemplates a process that involves both the employer and the qualified individual with a disability. Under this problem-solving approach, the employer should:

1. Analyze the job and identify its essential functions.
2. Discuss the precise job-related limitations with the disabled individual and inquire how these limitations could be overcome with a reasonable accommodation.
3. Identify potential accommodations and assess the effectiveness of each.
4. Consider the preference of the employee and select the accommodation that is most appropriate for the employee and the employer.

Bill Gunther needs dialysis treatment two days per week. Therefore, he can no longer work Monday through Friday. He can work the other three days that he is not undergoing dialysis. Bill can still perform the essential functions of his job as an accountant. He meets with his supervisor and they consider certain options: (1) Bill works only three days a week; (2) he comes in on the weekend to make up for the two days he misses; (3) he lengthens his other workdays, working an additional two hours each day. Bill and his supervisor agree that the third alternative is preferable. ■

WHAT AN EMPLOYER MUST DO TO REASONABLY ACCOMMODATE

There are many different methods for reasonably accommodating employees. What will be a reasonable accommodation in a particular case depends on the facts of that case. However, reasonable accommodation may include:

- Providing physical access to the application process, to the work site, and to the facilities used by the employees.
- Job restructuring.
- Modifying work schedules.
- Reassigning to a vacant position.
- Modifying employment policies.
- Acquiring or modifying equipment or devices.
- Adjusting or modifying examinations or training materials.
- Providing leave when necessary.
- Providing reserved parking.
- Assigning a person to help an employee, such as a page turner or travel companion.

Examples of Reasonable Accommodations

There are many devices available, some at a minimal cost, that can remove barriers to employment. The *Technical Assistance Manual* issued by the Equal Employment Opportunity Commission to assist employers in learning their obligations under the ADA, identifies, for example:

- Telecommunication devices that make it possible for the hearing impaired to use the telephone.

- Talking calculators that can be used by people with visual or reading disabilities.
- Speaker phones that can be used by persons with mobility impairments.

The manual also identifies examples of employees who have been accommodated at very reasonable cost:

- A clerk with limited use of her hands was provided a Lazy Susan file folder that enabled her to reach all materials needed for her job. Cost: $85.
- A person who had use of only one hand working in a food service position could perform all tasks except opening cans. She was provided with a one-handed can opener. Cost: $35.
- A phone headset allowed an insurance salesman with cerebral palsy to write while talking to clients. Rental cost: $6 per month.
- Purchase of a lightweight mop and a smaller broom enabled an employee with Down's syndrome and congenital heart problems to do his job. Cost: under $40.

Exercise 4.1

Answer the questions that follow each scenario. Explanations appear at the end of the book.

1. Larry Johnson is applying for a position as a math teacher. He has a B.S. in math but does not have the five years of teaching experience that is a requirement for the position. Larry tires easily because of the chemotherapy he receives for a cancer condition. Does the school system to which Larry is applying have an obligation to accommodate his fatigue? Why or why not? _____
_____
_____
_____
_____
_____

2. Peggy Joyce was the director of special events at a resort hotel for many years. In the last year, she developed a respiratory condition that makes it difficult for her to leave the controlled environment of her home. While she can plan menus and order supplies from her

home, she cannot make it to the hotel to perform the most significant aspect of her position; that is, supervising the employees the three days prior to each weekly event, meeting the sponsor of the events, and serving as the master of ceremonies. Her physical condition is expected to last for many years. Does the hotel have an obligation to accommodate her? Why or why not? _____

3. Melvin Rogers is an analyst in the claims department of an insurance company. He has been having some performance difficulties that he believes may be related to his hearing impairment. He will be having his performance review in two weeks. He has asked his employer if the company would provide a sign language interpreter at the review to help him understand the criticisms concerning his work. Does the company have an obligation to provide the interpreter? Why or why not? _____

4. Blaine Thomas is a manager of human resources who violated the trust placed in him by disclosing confidential medical information about three employees to other employees who did not need to know. When confronted with this conduct and advised that he was to be discharged, Blaine reported that he had been experiencing severe emotional problems lately and that he had been unable to control his behavior. He asked for another chance. However, Blaine failed to provide his employer with a letter from a psychiatrist or other mental health care provider supporting his version of the events. Does the employer have to accommodate Blaine by refraining from discharging him? Why or why not? _____

5. Mavis Healey, age 55, will be returning to work as a buyer for a national chain of department stores following a mild stroke. Her physician cleared her to return to work at her Chicago office

without limitation. Mavis has requested that the chain transfer her to an open position in its Miami operation and pay her relocation expenses. Does the chain have an obligation to grant this request? Why or why not? _____

_____

_____

6. Jake Diamond is an X-ray technician with diabetes. He must eat on a regular schedule and take insulin at set times each day. The other six X-ray technicians rotate their meal and break periods. Jake requested a variation from policy so that he could have regular meal and break periods. Does the hospital have to accommodate him? Why or why not? _____

_____

_____

Chapter Checkpoints

✓ The ADA requires employers to provide qualified applicants or employees with a reasonable accommodation if a disability prevents the individual from performing the essential functions of a job.

✓ Accommodations ensure equal opportunity in the application process and enable employees to perform essential functions and to enjoy equal benefits of employment.

✓ Reasonable accommodations may include modifications to the workplace such as making facilities accessible, job restructuring, acquiring equipment or devices, providing leaves of absence, and altering testing techniques.

✓ The employer deciding whether an accommodation is necessary should first decide whether the applicant or employee is disabled, whether he or she is otherwise qualified, and whether he or she can perform the essential functions of the job.

CHAPTER 5

Undue Hardship

This chapter will help you to:

- Identify under what circumstances an employer will *not* have an obligation to accommodate a qualified applicant or employee.

Jason Cummings is applying for a position as an usher at an off-Broadway theater. He has a disabling visual impairment that makes it extremely difficult for him to see in the dark. He requests that the theater keep the lights brighter during performances so that he can lead people to their seats. ■

Does the theater have an obligation to comply with Jason's request? Why or why not? _____

_____

An employer is not required to provide an accommodation that will impose an undue hardship on the operation of the employer's business. Undue hardship means significant difficulty or expense in or resulting from the accommodation. If a particular accommodation would impose an undue hardship, the employer should consider whether there are alternative accommodations that can be made.

Specifically, Section 102(b)(5) of the ADA provides that an employer need not provide a reasonable accommodation to a qualified applicant or employee if the employer can demonstrate that the accommodation would impose an undue hardship on the operation of the business. Section 101(10) defines undue hardship as follows:

(A) The term "undue hardship" means an action requiring significant difficulty or expense, when considered in light of the factors set forth in subparagraph (B).

(B) In determining whether an accommodation would impose an undue hardship on a covered entity, factors to be considered include:

   (i) the nature and cost of the accommodation needed under this Act;

   (ii) the overall financial resources of the facility or facilities involved in the provision of the reasonable accommodation; the number of persons employed at such facility; the effect on expenses and resources, or the impact otherwise of such accommodation upon the operation of the facility;

   (iii) the overall financial resources of the covered entity; the overall size of the business of a covered entity with respect to the number of its employees; the number, type, and location of its facilities; and

   (iv) the type of operation or operations of the covered entity, including the composition, structure, and functions of the workforce of such entity; the geographic separateness, administrative, or fiscal relationship of the facility or facilities in question to the covered entity.

HOW TO DETERMINE UNDUE HARDSHIP

In general, undue hardship refers to any accommodation that would be unduly costly, extensive, substantial, disruptive, or that would fundamentally alter the nature or operation of the business. Factors considered in determining whether an accommodation causes undue hardship include:

- The nature and cost of the accommodation.
- The financial resources of the facility making the accommodation.
- The overall financial resources of the employer, including the number, type, and location of its facilities and the number of employees.
- The type of operation of the employer, including the relationship of the facility to the employer.
- The impact of the accommodation upon the operation of the facility.

Whether an accommodation will cause an undue hardship depends on the facts of each case. What constitutes an undue hardship for a small employer may be more easily accomplished by an employer with a greater number of employees or more substantial assets. Additionally, what constitutes an undue hardship for an employer engaged in one type of business may not be an undue hardship for an employer in a different business.

Roy Baker is one of two salespersons at a national chain store selling computer equipment. Roy has asked for permission to work part-time, 20 hours per week, because a problem with varicose veins makes it difficult for him to be on his feet all day. The store has been unable to find anyone qualified to work part-time to fill in for Roy. Alice Bean, the other salesperson, is unable to handle the store by herself. The employer would be justified in claiming that the accommodation requested by Roy would be an undue hardship.

If the store was adjacent to a junior college whose major course of study was computers and whose 1,000 students frequently were looking for part-time work in the field, the employer would not be justified in claiming undue hardship.

If the store had 10 salespersons who worked overlapping shifts, the employer also would not be justified in claiming undue hardship. ■

Arthur Burns is a waiter at a large Orlando restaurant that also has an outdoor cafe. Since starting his job, Arthur always has been assigned to tables in the outdoor cafe. He now is suffering from a skin condition that requires that he refrain from being exposed to sunlight. He asks his employer to assign him to tables indoors. This accommodation would not present an undue hardship.

Suppose instead that Arthur is a waiter in a small cafe that is part of an Orlando department store. Arthur is the only waiter during his six-hour shift and handles all the tables, both indoors and outside. The only other cafe employee during his shift is the cook. Arthur asks that he work only the indoor tables and that the store hire an additional waiter to work his shift to handle the outside tables. The cost, with the employee benefits, would be an additional $15,000. The result would be different here; the accommodation could present an undue hardship.

Suppose Arthur asked the employer to put an awning over the outdoor tables to shield them from the sun and that he was able to find an awning manufacturer who would install the awning at a very moderate cost. If having an awning outside would change the nature of the business—and a valid argument could be made that it would—the employer would not be required to accommodate Arthur. ■

There are additional principles that employers should keep in mind when considering undue hardship:

1. An employer may consider the impact of the accommodation on other employees.

Marion Jones is part of a four-person team working on a six-month marketing project. Because of physical therapy she receives every afternoon, she requested that the team work 6:00 A.M. to 2:00 P.M. rather than 9:00 A.M. to 5:00 P.M. The employer may be in a position to contend that the requested accommodation presents an undue hardship. ■

2. An employer may not consider the impact on the morale of other employees.

Herb Adams requested a reserved parking spot near the plant entrance because of a back problem that affects his ability to walk. The employer cannot deny this request simply because other employees may be annoyed that Herb got a reserved spot. ■

3. If the cost of an accommodation presents an undue hardship, the employee must be given the option of providing the accommodation himself or herself or paying the portion of the cost that constitutes the undue hardship.

Bob Conti is visually impaired but knows of a computer designed to accommodate his impairment that will cost $15,000. Bob is seeking a position with a small real estate firm that does not have the funds to make that purchase, though it could contribute $5,000. Bob is qualified for the position. The employer probably can ask Bob to provide the computer or to contribute $10,000 to the purchase. ■

Exercise 5.1

Check those examples where the employer probably will be able to demonstrate that an accommodation constitutes an undue hardship. Explanatory answers are at the end of the book.

Undue Hardship

☐ 1. Alex Taggert is a hearing-impaired engineer. He requested that his firm provide a sign language interpreter for his two-hour, regularly scheduled monthly department meetings. The cost will be $75 per meeting. The firm has 350 employees at his location. The firm has been profitable of late.

☐ 2. Leslie Williams is HIV positive. He requested a transfer to an afternoon shift to accommodate medical appointments he has on occasional mornings. The afternoon supervisor does not want to work with Leslie because of his condition. The supervisor asked that the request for an accommodation be denied.

☐ 3. Ken Meade is one of five truck drivers for a shoe distributor. The drivers stock their trucks at the distributor's warehouse and deliver the merchandise to retail warehouses throughout a five-state region. Historically, the drivers have always loaded their own trucks. Because of a back condition, Ken asked his employer if his trucks could be loaded by the stock clerks who handle the goods in the warehouse. The stock clerks are willing to assist Ken but it would mean that one of them would have to devote approximately three hours a week to this effort.

☐ 4. Marilyn Baker is a buyer for a national chain of shoe stores. The buyers are required to travel extensively; she has developed an ear impairment that makes flying very painful. Marilyn requested that she be transferred to a position as an assistant buyer, a position that does not require travel. However, the chain historically has opened the assistant buyer position only to persons without any experience. Because Marilyn has 20 years of buying experience, she would not qualify under the chain's policy for a position as an assistant buyer.

☐ 5. Dennis Loren is a programmer for a brokerage firm. He participates in group therapy sessions from noon to 5:00 P.M. every workday. Accordingly, he requested a shift that runs from 8:00 P.M. to 4:00 A.M. To accommodate Dennis's request, his firm would be required to keep the office open all night. Because of the firm's remoteness and no security program, a night shift has never been considered.

Chapter Checkpoints

✓ The ADA does not require an employer to accommodate a disability if to do so would impose an undue hardship on the employer.

✓ Factors considered in deciding whether an accommodation causes an undue hardship include:

> The nature and cost of the accommodation.
>
> The financial resources of the employer and of the facility making the accommodation.
>
> The type of operation of the employer.
>
> The impact of the accommodation upon the operation of the facility.

✓ If the cost of an accommodation presents an undue hardship, the employee should be given the option of paying for the accommodation or contributing to its cost.

CHAPTER 6

Preemployment Inquiries

This chapter will help you to:

- Determine the kinds of preemployment inquiries that are permissible under the ADA.

Paula Phillips arrives at the office of Amy Donato, director of human resources, for a job interview. Paula is seeking a position as a building custodian. Amy notices that Paula is wearing a leg brace and thinks that the brace may cause problems in the performance of the custodian's duties. However, Amy knows of the ADA and is uncertain of the questions she may ask Paula. ■

What questions can Amy safely, under the ADA, ask Paula to ascertain whether she will be able to perform the essential duties of custodian?

PROHIBITED INQUIRIES

The ADA prohibits an employer from asking questions about an applicant's physical or mental condition during the interview process. Specifically, Section 102(c)(2)(A) of the ADA provides that, except as permitted as part of a preemployment medical examination conducted after an offer of employment is made,

> a covered entity shall not conduct a medical examination or make inquiries of a job applicant as to whether such applicant is an individual with a disability or as to the nature or severity of such disability.

The ADA includes this prohibition to preclude employers from screening out disabled applicants because of fears that they will not perform adequately, that they will not be accepted by their co-workers, that they will be reinjured at work, or that they will submit costly insurance claims. Accordingly, under the ADA, questions such as those stated below *cannot* be asked in an interview or on an employment application:

- Do you have any health problems?
- Have you ever been hospitalized?
- Have you ever had surgery?
- Are you taking any prescribed drugs?
- Have you ever been treated for a mental condition?
- Have you ever received disability or worker's compensation benefits?
- How many days were you absent from work because of illness last year?
- Have you ever seen a psychiatrist?
- How much alcohol do you consume?
- What kind of exercises do you do?

PERMISSIBLE INQUIRIES

While the ADA prohibits inquiries about an applicant's physical or mental condition, it permits inquiries about an applicant's ability to perform specific job functions. Section 102(c)(2)(B) of the ADA provides that "A covered entity may make preemployment inquiries into the ability of an applicant to perform job-related functions." Accordingly, questions such as those listed below do *not* violate the ADA when they relate to specific job-related functions:

- Can you arrive at work at 8:00 A.M.?
- Can you make deliveries around town?
- Can you perform cardiopulmonary resuscitation (CPR) on an adult patient?
- Can you operate a photocopy machine?
- Can you stock the grocery shelves?
- Can you make 10 visits to customers each week?

- Can you drive a truck?
- Can you type 65 words per minute?
- Can you work 40 hours each week?

PERMISSIBLE INQUIRIES FOR OBVIOUSLY DISABLED APPLICANTS

The ADA permits employers to ask applicants whether they can perform specific job-related tasks. If an applicant has a disability that is obvious to the interviewer or that would seem to impact on the applicant's ability to perform a job-related task, the ADA permits the employer to ask the applicant how he or she would perform the task.

Ken Levy, who uses a cane, applies for a position as a sales representative. The position requires the sales rep to make calls on customers and to carry a large sample bag. The interviewer can ask Ken how he would carry the samples to the customer. ■

Paul Ramondo applies for a position as a school librarian. He has the use of only one arm, a limitation that is visible to the interviewer. The interviewer can ask Paul to demonstrate how he would apply the book catalog number to the spine of a book. ■

Caution: If an applicant has a known disability but that disability does not have an impact on the ability to perform a job-related task, the interviewer may not ask for a demonstration of the function unless he asks all applicants for such a demonstration.

Lacy Thrasher, in a wheelchair, applies for a position as a bookkeeper. The interviewer cannot ask Lacy to demonstrate how she makes entries on a computer unless all applicants for that position are routinely asked to do so. ■

Susan Weider, in a wheelchair, applies for a position as a secretary. The interviewer can give Susan the typing test that all applicants are required to take. ■

An employer should keep some additional principles in mind when considering preemployment inquiries:

- An employer who uses an employment agency to recruit candidates may be liable along with the agency for violating the ADA if the agency makes prohibited preemployment inquiries.
- An employer should make sure that its in-house interviewers and any agency used to recruit employees are trained to know which inquiries are permissible under the ADA.
- While an employer may not inquire about a disability, it may make a job offer that is conditioned on a post-offer medical examination if it requires such an examination of all applicants for that job category.
- An employer may not ask an applicant whether he or she will require time off for medical treatment. The employer can advise the applicant that the position requires 40 hours of work per week and that he or she will be given two weeks' vacation and then can ask the applicant if he or she can fulfill that obligation.
- An employer may call a former employer for a reference on a job applicant. However, the employer may *not* ask questions that could not be asked of the applicant, such as did the applicant file any worker's compensation claims or miss any time from work due to illness.

Exercise 6.1

You are conducting an interview of an applicant for a stock clerk position. You notice that the applicant has a severe limp. Check the questions that you may ask the applicant. Explanatory answers are at the end of the book.

- [ ] 1. Do you expect your condition to cause you to take much time off?
- [ ] 2. How will you be able to bring boxes up from the basement?
- [ ] 3. How did you acquire the limp?
- [ ] 4. Can you stand for two hours at a time?
- [ ] 5. Did you sue anyone as a result of the condition that caused you to have the limp?
- [ ] 6. Does anyone in your family have a similar condition?
- [ ] 7. Is your leg painful?
- [ ] 8. How much were your medical expenses last year as a result of your leg problem?

Chapter Checkpoints

✓ The ADA prohibits an employer from asking questions about an applicant's physical or mental health during the interview process.

✓ The employer may ask the applicant questions about his or her ability to perform specific job-related functions.

✓ The employer should have written job descriptions for each position before advertising or interviewing for the position, so that the interviewer can ask about the applicant's ability to perform specific functions of the job.

✓ If an applicant has a known disability that impacts his or her ability to perform one of the position's essential functions, the employer may ask the applicant how he or she would perform the function.

CHAPTER 7
Medical Examinations

This chapter will help you to:
- Determine the conditions under which preemployment and postemployment medical examinations are permissible under the ADA.

PREEMPLOYMENT MEDICAL EXAMINATIONS

Dan Sweeney has been asked by his boss, the vice president of human resources, to establish a preemployment medical examination procedure that complies with the ADA. ■

Can Dan require that all applicants undergo a medical examination?

Can Dan limit testing to those applicants he feels may be suffering from a medical condition?

To whom can Dan give the results of any medical examinations?

After making a conditional job offer, an employer may require a preemployment medical examination. Section 102(c)(3) of the ADA provides that:

> A covered entity may require a medical examination after an offer of employment has been made to a job applicant and prior to the commencement of the employment duties of such applicant, and may condition an offer of employment on the results of such examination, if—

(A) all entering employees are subjected to such an examination regardless of disability;

(B) information obtained regarding the medical condition or history of the applicant is collected and maintained on separate forms and in separate medical files and is treated as a confidential medical record, except that—

   (i) supervisors and managers may be informed regarding necessary restrictions on the work or duties of the employee and necessary accommodations;

   (ii) first aid and safety personnel may be informed, when appropriate, if the disability might require emergency treatment; and

   (iii) government officials investigating compliance with this Act shall be provided relevant information on request; and

(C) the results of such examination are used only in accordance with this title.

An employer who uses preemployment, post-offer medical inquiries or medical examinations must be aware of the following principles:

1. An examination may be required only if all employees in a job category are subjected to the examination.

Ken Harris applies for a position in the machine shop of a cabinet manufacturer. He voluntarily discloses to the interviewer that he had a herniated disc three years ago. The employer may condition Ken's job offer on the satisfactory results of a medical examination only if it requires the examination of all employees in the machine shop. ∎

2. The examination required of all applicants may vary depending on the results of specific tests.

As part of the post-offer medical examination for employees in the machine shop, the physician listens to each applicant's heart with a stethoscope. When the physician hears a murmur while conducting the exam of one applicant, the physician orders an echocardiogram, a test that is not routinely done. He can order an exam not done on all applicants without violating the ADA. ∎

Under certain circumstances, employers can call for pre-employment and postemployment medical examinations.

3. Information from the medical examination must be maintained in separate medical files and treated as a confidential medical record.

Beth McDonough is manager of human resources for a small manufacturing company. When she receives reports from the preemployment physical examinations, she immediately files them in a locked cabinet for medical records. These reports never are placed in a personnel file. This is a required practice under the ADA. ■

4. A supervisor or manager may be informed only about restrictions or accommodations and *not* about actual test results or any diagnosed condition.

Jorge Sanchez received an offer to join the maintenance staff of a resort hotel. At his preemployment physical, the physician learns that Jorge has a skin condition that requires that he minimize his exposure to sunlight. Jorge's supervisor can be told that

Jorge needs to be assigned to indoor tasks. He must not be told about Jorge's skin condition. ■

WITHDRAWING A JOB OFFER

Suppose that an employer subjects an applicant to a post-offer medical examination and the employer learns that the applicant had a back injury three years earlier that severely restricts his motion and for which he is still receiving treatment. Can the employer withdraw the offer of employment?

The ADA provides that an offer of employment can be withdrawn in only limited circumstances:

1. If the employer can establish that the withdrawal of the offer is job related and consistent with business necessity.
2. If the employer can establish that the applicant poses a direct threat to health or safety (see Chapter 8).
3. If the employer can establish that no reasonable accommodation is available to enable the applicant to perform essential job functions.

Heather Wong applies for a position on a cruise ship. She undergoes a post-offer medical examination. It reveals that she will require surgery within a month for removal of a cancerous tumor. The surgery will require four to six weeks of recuperation and follow-up treatment. The cruise ship will be at sea for the next four months. The cruise line probably can withdraw Heather's offer of a job because there is no reasonable accommodation that can be made since Heather will be unavailable for almost half of the tour of duty. ■

An offer may not be withdrawn if the medical examination reveals only that there is some speculative risk of a future disabling problem. Nor may the employer withdraw an offer because of a concern about future insurance or worker's compensation claims.

Shirley Dunn applies for a position as a sales manager. She undergoes the post-offer medical examination; it reveals that she has an emotional condition for which she is on medication. The job offer may not be withdrawn because of a fear that Shirley will stop taking her medication and become unstable or violent. That risk is too speculative. ■

CONDUCTING THE PREEMPLOYMENT EXAMINATION

An employer who requires medical examinations as a condition of employment after a job offer is extended will be required to follow ADA guidelines on the conduct of the examination and the disclosure of the results of the examination.

- Prior to the examination, the physician should be provided with the job description or the essential functions of the job. The physician may then advise the employer as to the limitations of a particular candidate. The employer has the responsibility for deciding whether or not it is able to make a reasonable accommodation.
- All information obtained in the medical examination must be kept confidential. It must be kept in a separate medical file, *not* in a personnel file, and it should be left in the custody of an employee specifically designated to maintain those records.
- Supervisors and managers may be informed about work restrictions and accommodations.
- Safety personnel may be informed of the results of the medical examination so that they are prepared to respond to an emergency.

POSTEMPLOYMENT MEDICAL EXAMINATIONS

Dan Sweeney's boss, the vice president of human resources, says that the preemployment medical examination program is working so well that he wants Dan to implement a program for employees. ∎

Can Dan require that all employees undergo medical examinations if there is a problem with performance? _____

Can Dan require all employees who have been out ill for a week to undergo a medical examination before returning to work? _____

The ADA imposes greater restrictions on medical examinations of employees than on medical examinations of applicants. An employer may subject an employee to a medical examination or inquiry only where the examination or inquiry is job related and consistent with business necessity.

Ben Lee is frequently absent, performing poorly and exhibiting symptoms of alcohol abuse. Ben's employer may suggest a medical examination. ■

David Shaffer, an accountant, returns to work following surgery to remove a benign tumor. David's employer may not subject David to a medical examination because an examination is not job related or a business necessity under these circumstances. ■

A medical examination may also be required if the employee requests an accommodation due to a disability. The examination may be conducted to determine if there is a disability and if an accommodation is appropriate.

Sally Keefe is a quality assurance nurse at a Minneapolis nursing home owned and operated by a firm that owns other nursing homes around the country. Sally asks her employer to relocate her to Arizona because of a lung condition that precludes her from continuing to live in Minneapolis. The employer can ask for a medical examination to verify the disability and the need for accommodation. ■

■ Exercise 7.1

Check those employment practices that would be appropriate under the ADA. Explanatory answers are at the end of the book.

☐ 1. John Reynolds has been offered a position as a short-order cook in the cafeteria of a large company. John is asked to undergo a medical exam. No employees other than kitchen workers are required to submit to such exams.

☐ 2. As a result of her preemployment medical exam, it is discovered that Maria Lopez has epilepsy. Maria's supervisor is informed of her condition so that she will be in a position to assist Maria in the event of a seizure at work.

☐ 3. Laura Price applies for a position as a production manager at a manufacturing plant. After receiving an offer of employment, Laura is scheduled for the preemployment physical exam given to all employees. Laura objects to undergoing the exam. Lyle Jacobs, human resources manager, tells the president of the company that the ADA prohibits them from withdrawing Laura's offer of employment.

☐ **4.** Les Unger received an offer of employment for a position as a securities analyst. During his preemployment medical examination, the physician discovered that Les had an ulcer. The firm withdrew the offer of employment because of concern that the ulcer would worsen and Les might be unable to perform his duties.

☐ **5.** Louis Hernandez was employed as a security guard at a manufacturing facility. He was out of work for several months due to a home accident that resulted in a permanent loss of mobility in one arm. When he is able to return to work, his employer asks that he submit to a medical examination.

Chapter Checkpoints

✓ An employer may require a preemployment medical examination only of those applicants to whom a conditional offer of employment has been made.

✓ If an employer uses preemployment medical examinations, it must require that all employees within a job category undergo the examination.

✓ Information from preemployment medical examinations must be maintained in separate medical files and treated as a confidential medical record.

✓ An offer of employment can be withdrawn only if the withdrawal is job related and consistent with business necessity, if the employer can establish that the applicant poses a direct threat to the health and safety of himself/herself or others, or if no reasonable accommodation is available to enable the applicant to perform essential job functions.

✓ A medical examination of an employee may be conducted if it is job related and consistent with business necessity or to determine if there is a disability and if an accommodation is appropriate.

CHAPTER 8

Qualification Standards and Selection Criteria

This chapter will help you to:

- Identify qualification standards and selection criteria that are permissible under the ADA.

Craig Windsor applies for a position as a security guard at a manufacturing facility. A requirement of the position is that the employee have a valid driver's license. While the security guard does not have to drive, the employer includes the requirement because it believes that having a nonrevoked driver's license assures that the applicant is of upstanding character. Craig does not have a driver's license because he has epilepsy and believes that it is not safe for him to drive. ■

Can the employer apply its qualification standard to bar Craig from the security guard position? Why or why not?

QUALIFICATION STANDARDS

The ADA prohibits discriminaition against otherwise qualified disabled persons who can perform the essential functions of a job, with or without reasonable accommodation. However, an employer will *not* be deemed to have discriminated if it can show that an employee or applicant could not meet certain selection criteria. Section 103(a) of the ADA provides that

> It may be a defense to a charge of discrimination under this Act that an alleged application of qualification standards, tests, or selection criteria that screen out or tend to screen out or otherwise deny a job or benefit to an

individual with a disability has been shown to be job related and consistent with business necessity, and such performance cannot be accomplished by reasonable accommodation, as required under this title.

Employers routinely establish job qualifications relating to education, work experience, and licenses or certification. The ADA does not alter the employer's right to set those qualifications. It does, however, alter that right if those standards screen out disabled employees.

Impact on Disabled Persons

While the ADA does not prohibit employers from establishing job-related qualification standards, it will require that they be *job related* and *consistent with business necessity* if they screen out individuals with a disability or a class of persons with disabilities.

Family Hospital has as a requirement for an emergency medical technician that he or she be able to perform CPR on an adult patient. That requirement is job related and consistent with business necessity.

It is illegal to discriminate against disabled employees who can perform essential job functions.

Family Hospital has a requirement for a nurse at its outpatient clinic that he or she be able to perform CPR on an adult patient. That requirement is job related but not consistent with business necessity because the nurse in that position has never been required to perform CPR as there is always a physician available.

Family Hospital has as a requirement for a nurse in its pediatric ward that he or she be able to perform CPR on an adult patient. That requirement is neither job related nor consistent with a business necessity since the nurse will not be treating adult patients. ■

Direct Threat

An employer may require as a qualification standard that an employee not pose a direct threat to the health and safety of himself/herself or others. Section 103(b) of the ADA provides that the "qualification standards" that may be established by an employer include "a requirement that an individual shall not pose a direct threat to the health or safety of other individuals in the workplace." Section 1630.2(r) of the ADA regulations makes clear that a "direct threat" also exists if the individual presents a risk of harm to himself/herself. However, if an employer contends that an individual poses a direct threat, it must be prepared to show that:

1. There is a specific risk.
2. The risk is of substantial harm.
3. The risk is current rather than remote or speculative.
4. The employer's concern about the risk is based on objective evidence and not on fear or stereotypes.
5. There is no reasonable accommodation that can sufficiently reduce the threat to acceptable standards.

Marling Sams receives an offer of a position as a bus driver. During his orientation, he mentions that he currently is in an alcohol rehabilitation program. The employer can withdraw the offer without violating the ADA if the employer believes that the risk that Marling's ability to drive may be impaired is not too remote and therefore that the risk is a substantial one. ■

Jerome Brown applies for a promotion to city editor of a newspaper. The chief editor knows that Jerome was treated several years ago for emotional problems and believes that the position may be too stressful for Jerome's emotional well-being. The chief editor cannot refuse the promotion without some medical evidence that Jerome should not be subjected to stress. In this case, the chief editor does not have sufficient evidence of risk. ∎

The ADA provides special rules for employees engaged in the handling of food. The Center for Disease Control of the Public Health Services issues a list (which periodically changes) of infectious diseases transmitted through the handling of foods. If any employee has such a disease, the employer must determine if a reasonable accommodation is possible. If it is not, an employer, pursuant to Section 103(d)(2) of the ADA, "may refuse to assign or continue to assign such individual to a job involving food handling." HIV and AIDS are not on that list.

SELECTION CRITERIA

The ADA requires employers to modify their selection procedures to accommodate disabled applicants. Section 1630.11 of the ADA regulations provides that

> It is unlawful for a covered entity to fail to select and administer tests concerning employment in the most effective manner to ensure that, when a test is administered to a job applicant or employee who has a disability that impairs sensory, manual or speaking skills, the test results accurately reflect the skills, aptitude or whatever other factor of the applicant or employee that the test purports to measure, rather than reflecting the impaired sensory, manual or speaking skills of such employee or applicant (except where such skills are the factors that the test purports to measure).

Joy Hurley applies for a position as marketing manager for a computer company. The company requires that all of its employees take a multiple-choice, written personality profile exam. Because Joy is dyslexic, the company may have to modify its testing procedures to permit Joy to take the exam orally. ∎

Laura Chen applies for a position as a proofreader. The company gives all applicants a proofreading exam which they are required to complete in 30 minutes. Even though

Laura is dyslexic, the company can give her the test and ask her to complete it in 30 minutes, since her ability to read quickly and accurately is what the test is designed to measure. ■

The ADA places some responsibility for the accommodation on the applicant. The applicant should request an accommodation prior to the administration of the test or as soon as the applicant becomes aware of the need for an accommodation.

Exercise 8.1

Check those situations that involve violations of the ADA. Explanatory answers are at the end of the book.

☐ 1. Barry Douglas applies for a position as an ambulance driver. One of the requirements for this position is that the employee be in excellent health.

☐ 2. Kevin Feeney applies for a position as a waiter at an exclusive resort hotel. One of the requirements for that position is that the employee not pose a direct threat to himself or others.

☐ 3. Jessica Chaplan applies for a position as a bus driver. One of the requirements for that position is that the employee have 20-20 vision.

☐ 4. Ralph Wainwrit applies for a position as a hospital orderly. The hospital requires all applicants for the position to demonstrate lifting patients out of a hospital bed and placing them on a stretcher.

☐ 5. Christopher Peters applies for a position as an engineer. He has AIDS. He is denied the position since his AIDS poses a direct threat to members of the engineering department.

☐ 6. Lee Richard applies for a position as a piano player in a hotel lounge. He is visually impaired. The hotel tests his musical abilities with their usual requirement of playing from the sheet of music provided.

Chapter Checkpoints

✓ Employers may establish job qualifications relating to education, work experience, and licenses or certification.

✓ The ADA prohibits employers from establishing qualifications that screen out disabled individuals unless the standards are job related and consistent with business necessity.

✓ Employers do not need to accommodate individuals who pose a direct threat to the health and safety of themselves or others, but they will be required to establish a specific risk of substantial harm that is current, that is based on objective evidence, and that cannot be reasonably accommodated.

✓ Employers will be required to modify their testing procedures for disabled applicants except in those instances where the test is designed to measure a skill affected by the disability.

CHAPTER 9

Drugs and Alcohol

This chapter will help you to:

- See how the ADA handles drug and alcohol issues.

Janice Bailer, manager of the claims department, has been struggling for months with one of her employees, Don Smith, a claims representative. Don has been absent frequently and his performance is erratic even when he is present. Despite repeated warnings and counseling sessions, Don has failed to improve. Janice has a meeting with Don to advise him that he is being terminated. Then Don blurts out that he is addicted to cocaine. ■

Can Janice still discharge Don? What if Don blurts out that he has a problem with alcohol? Does that require a different result?

EXCLUSION FOR ILLEGAL DRUG USE

The ADA excludes from its protection applicants or employees who currently use illegal drugs. Section 104(a) of the ADA provides that, for purposes of Title I,

> the term "qualified individual with a disability" shall not include any employee or applicant who is currently engaging in the illegal use of drugs, when the covered entity acts on the basis of such use.

There is no such exclusion for applicants or employees who use alcohol. Accordingly, the ADA treats drug and alcohol use differently. An individual currently engaging in the illegal use of drugs is not entitled to the protections of the ADA; an individual who uses alcohol is entitled to those protections.

Bob Worth is a salesman at a lumberyard who occasionally makes deliveries to customers. When using the company van to make a delivery, he hits a parked car, causing damage to the van and the car. Bob is questioned by his manager and admits that he had been using marijuana at the time of the accident. The manager can make a decision to discharge Bob without considering ADA implications.

Suppose instead that, when questioned by his manager, Bob states that he had been drinking several days earlier, that he had been upset about such conduct, and that he has an alcohol problem that he has been trying to beat. Now, in considering the appropriate cause of action, since Bob is disabled under the ADA, the manager may have to consider whether the lumberyard can accommodate this disability. Perhaps Bob needs a leave of absence to enter a treatment program. ∎

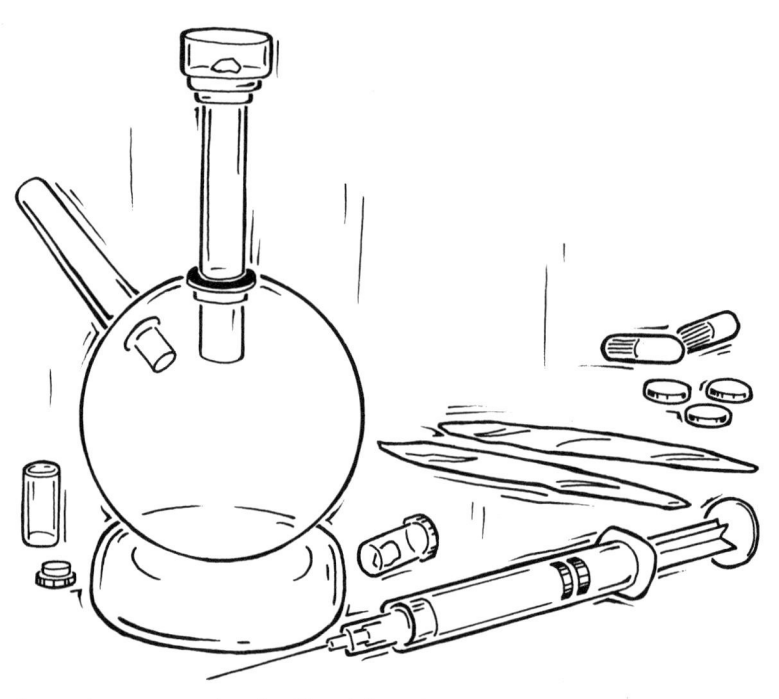

An employee currently using illegal drugs is *not* protected by the ADA.

Limits to Exclusion for Illegal Drug Use

Although an applicant or employee who currently uses illegal drugs will not be considered a qualified individual with a disability, there are limits to the exclusion from coverage under the ADA. The ADA makes clear that the exclusion of illegal drug use does not apply to an individual who:

- Successfully completed a supervised drug rehabilitation program and is no longer engaging in the illegal use of drugs.
- Is participating in a supervised rehabilitation program and is no longer engaging in use.
- Is erroneously regarded as engaging in illegal drug use.

The ADA also makes clear that employers can maintain drug testing programs without violating the act. Section 104(d)(2) of the ADA provides that

> Nothing in this title shall be construed to encourage, prohibit, or authorize the conducting of drug testing for the illegal use of drugs by job applicants or employees or making employment decisions based on such test results.

Sharon Taylor begins work as a nurse supervisor at a nursing home. During her orientation, she advises the director of nursing that she will need to leave the facility on time at the end of her shift because she is in a drug rehabilitation program that meets three evenings a week. The ADA prohibits the manager from withdrawing the offer of employment because the manager fears that Sharon will have a relapse. ■

ACTIONS THE EMPLOYER MAY TAKE

The ADA, in Section 104(c), sets out certain actions that an employer may take with respect to drugs and alcohol in the workplace. These include:

- The employer may prohibit the illegal use of drugs and the use of alcohol at the workplace.
- The employer may require that employees shall not be under the influence of alcohol or drugs at the workplace.
- The employer may require that employees conform to the requirements established under the Drug-Free Workplace Act of 1988.

- The employer may hold an employee who uses illegal drugs or alcohol to the same qualification standards for employment or job performance and behavior shown by other employees, even if any unsatisfactory behavior is related to drug use or alcoholism.

Employers may also attempt to limit smoking in the workplace, despite the potential for claims that an individual is addicted to nicotine and thus is disabled. Section 1630.16(d) of ADA regulations provides that an employer may prohibit or impose restrictions on smoking in places of employment.

Exercise 9.1

Check those persons who may be considered disabled under the ADA. Explanatory answers are at the end of the book.

- ☐ 1. Jennifer Lewis, a nurse, developed an addiction to valium prescribed by the physician treating her for back spasms.
- ☐ 2. Reggie Davis, a hotel food and beverage supervisor, uses cocaine. He took a leave of absence for a month in an attempt to get the drug use under control, but he did not participate in any formal rehabilitation program.
- ☐ 3. Alex Caine, a plant foreman, has been acting strangely. His eyes are red and dilated and he appears manic at times. The plant manager believes that Alex is using drugs, but Alex is not.
- ☐ 4. Marsha White, a buyer, had a drug problem a year ago. She is attending a rehabilitation program, but she recently admitted to her supervisor that she is using marijuana again.
- ☐ 5. Glen Williamson, a medical equipment sales representative, is an alcoholic. He has been through three rehabilitation programs but none has been successful.

Chapter Checkpoints

✓ Individuals who currently use illegal drugs are not protected by the ADA.

✓ The exclusion of protection does not apply to individuals who are in a rehabilitation program, who were successfully rehabilitated, or who are erroneously regarded as engaging in illegal drug use.

✓ Individuals who suffer from alcoholism will be considered disabled under the ADA.

CHAPTER 10
Filing Charges and Available Remedies

This chapter will help you to:
- Understand how a charge of discrimination under the ADA is filed and processed.
- Discover what remedies are available to victims of discrimination under the ADA.

Donald Brown was the executive director of a nonprofit organization. He was fired after the Board of Trustees learned that he had been diagnosed with cancer. He has been earning $100,000 annually, but has been unable to find a position since his discharge last year. He filed a charge of discrimination under the ADA, seeking to recover $100,000 per year for each year until he finds new employment, in addition to damages for his emotional distress, recovery of the costs of seeing a psychiatrist, and punitive damages. ∎

Can Donald recover all of the damages he seeks? Why or why not?

_____
_____

The remedies for a violation of the ADA are those available under Title VII of the Civil Rights Act of 1964, as amended by the Civil Rights Act of 1991. To bring a claim under the ADA, the applicant or employee who believes he is a victim of discrimination must file a charge of discrimination with the EEOC within 180 days of the date of the event which allegedly was unlawful, or 300 days if there is also a state agency which processes discrimination claims.

An individual wanting to bring an action for a violation of the ADA initiates the action by filing a charge of discrimination with the EEOC or with the state agency that handles discrimination claims. A charge will include information such as the applicant's or employee's name and address, the employer's name and address, the basis of the alleged unlawful discrimination, the date of the act, and the details of what happened.

Glenn Pinochet filed a typical charge with the EEOC:

> On November 15, I applied for a position as a science editor with ABC Books, a publisher of school textbooks. I have 10 years of experience in that field. I believe that I was denied the job because I am hearing impaired. I understand that the applicant who was hired has only two years of general editorial experience. She is not hearing impaired. ∎

FILING THE ADA CHARGE

The 180-day time clock (or 300-day time clock, if a state agency also exists) for filing the charge of discrimination generally runs from the date the adverse employment decision is communicated to the applicant or employee. That may be a date that is prior to the effective date of the action of which the applicant or employee complains.

Betty Whiteside is a production assistant at a television network. She missed three months of work last year due to a circulatory problem. On January 15, she is advised that she will be laid off on March 15 as part of a reduction in force. Betty thinks that she was selected for layoff solely because her employer believes that she will be out on leave again due to her illness. The time for filing the charge runs from January 15, the date the layoff is communicated to Betty. The time does not run from March 15. ∎

When the applicant or employee files a charge of discrimination due to a disability, he or she may also include in the charge any other claims of discrimination that he or she may have.

Celia Martinez, the assistant manager of a hotel, was denied a promotion to the position of manager. She believes that a factor in that decision was the loss of hearing she suffered which required that she use a hearing aid. She also thinks that the owners of the hotel were troubled by the fact that she is a woman and Hispanic. When Celia files her charge of discrimination with the Equal Employment Opportunity Commission

Once a discrimination suit is filed, the case may be brought before a judge or jury.

(EEOC), she can claim discrimination based on sex, national origin, and disability all at the same time. ∎

PROCESSING THE CHARGE OF DISCRIMINATION

The EEOC processes all charges of discrimination that it receives. In general, that processing includes four steps:

1. The EEOC notifies the employer that a charge was filed, sends the employer the charge, and asks for a response from the employer to the allegations made.
2. The EEOC reviews the charge and the response and may request that additional information be supplied.
3. The EEOC may request that the parties appear for a fact-finding conference at which additional evidence can be obtained or the possibility of settlement discussed.
4. After the completion of its review, the EEOC issues a Letter of Determination, advising the parties that it did or did not find reasonable cause to believe that discrimination occurred.

If the EEOC finds no cause to believe discrimination occurred, it will issue a right to sue letter advising the charging party that, although the

EEOC will not proceed, he or she has the right to initiate a lawsuit but that he or she must do so within 90 days of receiving the letter.

If the EEOC finds cause to believe that discrimination occurred, it will attempt to obtain a resolution through conciliation. If that is not successful, the EEOC may bring a suit on behalf of the charging party. The party also may ask the EEOC to issue a right to sue letter so that he or she may initiate his or her own lawsuit.

PROVING DISCRIMINATION IN A LAWSUIT

An individual who brings an action for discrimination under the ADA generally brings it in a state or federal court in the state in which he or she lives or was employed. Although there may be some variation in the proof required, the case of discrimination usually involves the following burdens of proof:

First, the applicant or employee has the burden of establishing a prima facie case of discrimination—that is, (1) that he or she is an otherwise qualified individual with a disability who can perform the essential functions of the job, with or without reasonable accommodation; and (2) that an adverse employment action was taken with respect to him or her.

Dean Murray was laid off on July 2 by Ace Beverage Distributors. He was the only management employee laid off at that time. Dean had been in a serious automobile accident six months earlier and was due to be readmitted to the hospital for more surgery later in the summer. Dean makes out a prima facie case of discrimination by showing that he was disabled but able to perform the essential functions of the job, that he was laid off, and that individuals without a disability were not laid off. ■

Second, after the applicant or employee makes out a prima facie case of discrimination, the employer then has the burden of articulating a legitimate business reason for the adverse employment decision.

Ace Beverage Distributors demonstrates at trial that Dean was manager of its fruit juice product line, that effective July 2 it was terminating that product line, and that it also laid off at that time all seven nonmanagement employees who worked on that product line. Ace has satisfied its burden of articulating a legitimate business reason for the layoff. ■

Third, if the employer can articulate a legitimate business reason for the action, the applicant or employee then has the burden of proving that the legitimate business reason articulated by the employer is a pretext—that is, a fabrication of a legitimate reason.

Dean proves that, on July 2, Ace also ended its soft drinks product line and laid off the 14 nonmanagement employees who worked that line. However, Stuart Bailer, the manager of that line was not laid off. Ace reassigned Stuart to its alcoholic beverage product line which recently lost some management personnel. Stuart does not suffer from a disability.

Additionally, Dean will testify that at recent management meetings, the president of Ace bemoaned the skyrocketing health insurance costs and said that the company should strive to hire healthy people who would not make insurance claims.

Dean has met his burden of establishing a pretext. ■

If the employee has evidence of pretext, a judge or jury will have to decide after hearing the evidence which of the witnesses it believes and which version of events is more likely than not to be true.

RECOVERABLE DAMAGES

Applicants or employees who prevail in an action charging discrimination under the ADA can recover the following as damages: back pay, reinstatement or front pay, restored benefits, and attorneys' fees and costs. They can also recover compensatory and punitive damages in cases of intentional discrimination. Compensatory damages are what applicants or employees can recover for emotional distress and out-of-pocket monetary losses—not including lost back pay, benefits, front pay, or attorney's fees and costs—that the employee or applicant has incurred as a result of the discrimination. Punitive damages are monetary awards given the employee or applicant for the willful disregard of the law on the part of the employer.

There is no limitation on the amount of damages that an employee or applicant can be awarded with respect to lost back pay, front pay, benefits, and attorneys' fees and costs. The amount of compensatory and punitive damages that can be awarded, however, are limited, depending on the size of the employer. Those limits are:

- If the employer has less than 101 employees, compensatory and punitive damages may not exceed $50,000.
- If the employer has less than 201 employees, compensatory and punitive damages may not exceed $100,000.
- If the employer has less than 501 employees, compensatory and punitive damages may not exceed $200,000.
- If the employer has more than 500 employees, compensatory and punitive damages may not exceed $300,000.

Maura Casey was fired on June 1 after she asked her employer, United Genetics, which employs 175 employees, to accommodate her need for time off to undergo disc surgery and recuperation. She had been earning $30,000 per year as an assistant laboratory manager. She was out of work for two years when her case came to trial, having been unable to obtain other employment until just prior to trial. She finally obtained a job in California, paying $25,000 a year. At trial, Maura seeks to recover:

Back pay:	$60,000. Her lost wages of $30,000 per year for two years.
Restored benefits:	$8,400, representing the $350 per month for 24 months (two years) that Maura paid to replace her health insurance until such time as she was covered by her new employer.
Front pay:	$25,000. $5,000 per year from the date of the trial forward (at least five years) to compensate her for the reduced earnings at her new employment.
Compensatory damages:	$33,000. Maura spent $5,000 looking for a new job and $5,000 in relocating to California for the job she

eventually obtained. She also incurred $3,000 in uncovered medical expenses for visits to a psychiatrist to deal with the emotional distress she suffered when she was discharged and seeks $20,000 to compensate her for that distress.

Punitive damages: Damages for the willful violation of the ADA.

Attorneys' costs and fees: Recovery of the costs and fees charged by her attorney for prosecuting the action.

If Maura can prove that she was unlawfully discriminated against, she can recover the full amounts of back pay, restored benefits, front pay, and attorneys' costs and fees that she seeks as there is no limitation on these amounts.

Her compensatory and punitive damages cannot exceed $100,000 since her employer employs less than 201 employees. Therefore, she can recover the $33,000 compensatory damages she seeks, but only up to $67,000 in punitive damages ($33,000 + $67,000 = $100,000). ∎

Exercise 10.1

Indicate on the corresponding blank whether the outcome of each of the scenarios is true or false. Explanatory answers are at the end of the book.

_____ 1. Carlos Medina sought a promotion to a supervisory position within the engineering firm that employed him. On September 1, he was told that he would not get the promotion because management feared that additional duties might cause his medical condition, a bleeding ulcer, to worsen. One month later, he files a charge of discrimination with the EEOC. He can pursue his claim.

_____ 2. Bill Holz was refused a position as a stockbroker because he had been hospitalized for depression several years earlier. His lawyer brought suit alleging a violation of the ADA. He never filed a charge of discrimination with the EEOC or the state agency. He can proceed with the court action anyway.

_____ 3. Andy Luzzo was discharged from his $40,000 per year position as an office manager because his employer thought he had a problem with alcohol. He got a job one year later but the position pays only $20,000. In his lawsuit, which was filed on time, alleging a violation of the ADA, he seeks to recover $40,000 in back wages for the year he was unemployed and $20,000 per year as front pay for each year that he is earning less than he had been. He may be able to recover that amount.

_____ 4. Lenora Jones was suffering from a serious kidney problem. Upon her return to work following a three-month absence, her employer said that she could continue to work but that they could no longer afford to keep her on health insurance. It took Lenora's lawyer several months to remedy that problem. In her timely lawsuit alleging a violation of the ADA, she seeks to recover for emotional distress. She may recover that.

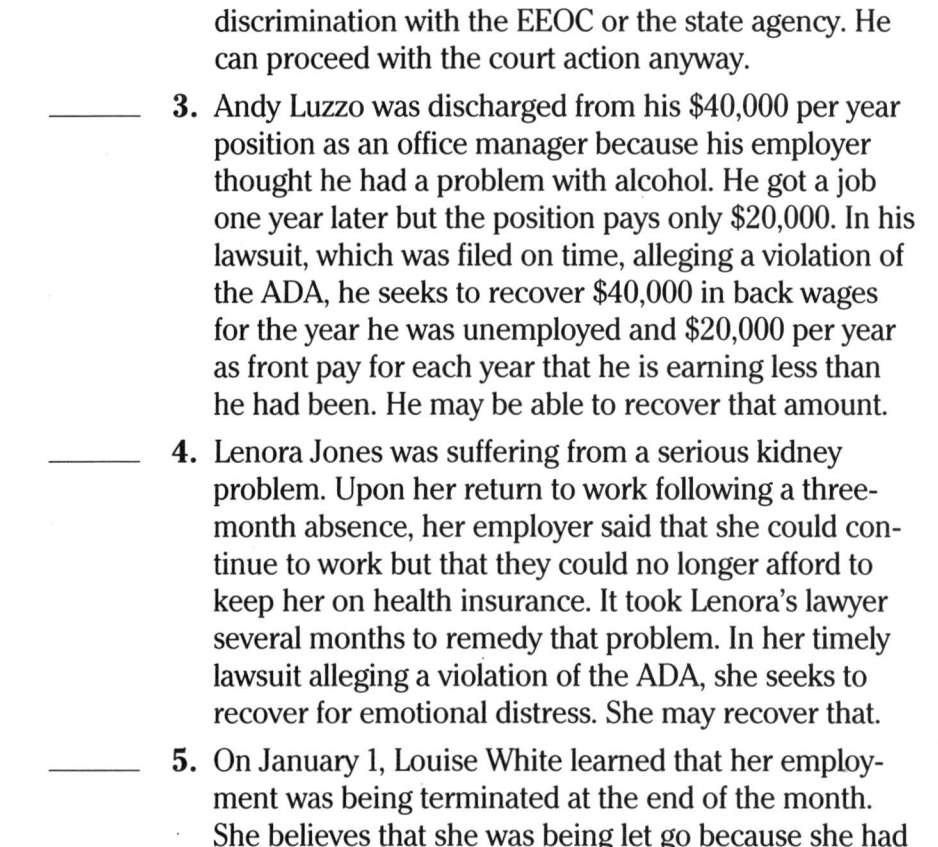

_____ 5. On January 1, Louise White learned that her employment was being terminated at the end of the month. She believes that she was being let go because she had emphysema. She filed a charge of discrimination with the EEOC on November 15. She can pursue her claim.

Chapter Checkpoints

- ✓ An applicant or employee who believes he or she is a victim of discrimination can file a charge of discrimination with the EEOC or a state human resources agency.

- ✓ The ADA requires that a charge be filed within 180 days of notification of the event of which the applicant or employee complains, or 300 days if there is also a state agency that processes discrimination claims.

- ✓ An employer will be required to offer evidence of a legitimate business reason for the employment decision at issue.

- ✓ An applicant or employee who establishes unlawful discrimination can recover various elements of damages including lost wages, out-of-pocket expenses and emotional distress (compensatory damages), punitive damages, and attorneys' costs and fees.

Postscript

You should now have a better understanding of the mechanics of the ADA. With this understanding of the ADA's terms and principles, you should be better able to analyze the factual situations that arise in your workplace to determine appropriate courses of action. While you may need to consult with an attorney in particular situations, in general, you should be performing a five-step analysis of situations in your workplace to arrive at a result that is consistent with the ADA:

1. Is the individual disabled?
2. Is he or she otherwise qualified for the position?
3. Can he or she perform the essential functions of the position, with or without reasonable accommodation?
4. Does the reasonable accommodation present an undue hardship?
5. Is the individual a direct threat to himself/herself or others?

The ADA was designed to permit entry of 43 million Americans into the work force. The wise employer recognizes that the ADA provides an opportunity to add untapped talent into the labor market, that everyone will benefit from that new talent, and that infusion of new workers is enhanced when employees understand the ADA, its purpose, and its provisions. If you appropriately train your employees and your recruiters and if you analyze the situations that arise in your workplace in light of what you have learned in this book, the goals of the ADA can be achieved.

Post-Test

Congratulations! You have just taken another important step in your professional development by completing *The* Americans with Disabilities Act: *What Supervisors Need to Know*.

This post-test is provided as a means of reinforcing the material you have just covered. If you have difficulty with any questions, you can refer to the answer key at the bottom of page 82.

Approximate time to complete: 15 minutes.

INSTRUCTIONS: Circle the letter of the correct answer.

1. An employee who claims to have been denied a promotion due to a disability can recover damages for which of the following?
    a. Wages lost when she failed to get the promotion.
    b. Attorneys' fees in pursuing a claim of discrimination.
    c. Punitive damages.
    d. All of the above.

2. Which of the following is not a disability under the ADA?
    a. Arthritis.
    b. Emotional illness.
    c. Cosmetic disfigurcmcnt.
    d. Normal pregnancy.

3. Which of the following is not true about the essential function of a job?
    a. The position exists to perform that function.
    b. There are only a limited number of employees available to perform that function.
    c. The function is so specialized that the incumbent is hired for his expertise or ability to perform that function.
    d. The function must be performed on a daily basis.

4. "Reasonable accommodation" under the ADA may include which of the following?
   a. Job restructuring.
   b. Modifying employment policies.
   c. Reassignment to a vacant position.
   d. All of the above.

5. Which of the following is an inappropriate action to take in response to an employee's request for an accommodation of a disability?
   a. Assessing various means to accommodate a disability.
   b. Asking the employee for medical verification of the need for accommodation.
   c. Denying the request because it would require modifying company policy.
   d. Considering the cost of the accommodation.

6. A factor *not* considered in determining whether an accommodation constitutes an undue hardship is
   a. the financial resources of the facility making the accommodation.
   b. the nature and cost of the accommodation.
   c. the opinion of the employer.
   d. the type of operation of the employer.

7. When interviewing an applicant who is hearing impaired for a position as a secretary, which of the following questions can the human resources manager ask?
   a. How long have you been hearing impaired?
   b. Have you ever had any problems at work as a result of your impairment?
   c. How would you be able to take phone messages?
   d. Does your hearing impairment cause you to lose any time from work?

8. ABC Company plans to do preemployment testing of certain categories of employees. Which of the following would be an acceptable category?

   a. All employees over age 55.

   b. All employees who appear to be in less than excellent health.

   c. All employees who have never before held a full-time job.

   d. All salaried employees.

9. Which of the following would *not* constitute prohibited discrimination under the ADA?

   a. Refusing to allow an employee with a heart condition to work overtime.

   b. Disciplining an employee with a disability for repeatedly failing to arrive at work on time where the failure is unrelated to the disability.

   c. Asking an employee with a cosmetic disfigurement to refrain from greeting customers.

   d. Paying an employee with a back condition less because he is unable to lift the heaviest packages in the mailroom.

10. Which of the following is *not* required by the ADA?

    a. Promoting employees without regard to their health.

    b. Having social functions that are accessible by disabled persons.

    c. Giving a preference in hiring to persons with disabilities.

    d. Modifying leave policies to accommodate disabled employees.

11. Which of the following would the employer be required to show if he plans to deny a job to an applicant because he believes that the applicant poses a direct threat to others?

    a. That the applicant has a condition that is contagious.

    b. That co-workers are afraid to have the applicant at the workplace.

    c. That the applicant presents a current specific risk of substantial harm.

    d. That the applicant will require time off from work for medical treatment.

12. Which of the following is not protected by the ADA?
    a. An employee currently using illegal drugs.
    b. An employee addicted to prescribed tranquilizers.
    c. A former illegal drug user, currently in a supervised rehabilitation program.
    d. An employee who is an alcoholic.

ANSWER KEY

1. d 2. d 3. d 4. d 5. c 6. c 7. c 8. d 9. b 10. c 11. c 12. a

Title I of the Americans with Disabilities Act of 1990

Section 1. Short Title; Table of Contents.

(a) Short title.—This Act may be cited as the "Americans with Disabilities Act of 1990".

(b) Table of contents.—The table of contents is as follows:

Sec. 1. Short title; table of contents.

Sec. 2. Findings and purposes.

Sec. 3. Definitions.

Title I—Employment

Sec. 101. Definitions.

Sec. 102. Discrimination.

Sec. 103. Defenses.

Sec. 104. Illegal use of drugs and alcohol.

Sec. 105. Posting notices.

Sec. 106. Regulations.

Sec. 107. Enforcement.

Sec. 108. Effective date.

Title II—Public Services

Subtitle A—Prohibition Against Discrimination and Other Generally Applicable Provisions

Sec. 201. Definition.

Sec. 202. Discrimination.

Sec. 203. Enforcement.

Sec. 204. Regulations.

Sec. 205. Effective date.

Subtitle B—Actions Applicable to Public Transportation Provided by Public Entities Considered Discriminatory

Part I—Public Transportation Other Than by Aircraft or Certain Rail Operations

Sec. 221. Definitions.

Sec. 222. Public entities operating fixed route systems.

Sec. 223. Paratransit as a complement to fixed route service.

Sec. 224. Public entity operating a demand responsive system.

Sec. 225. Temporary relief where lifts are unavailable.

Sec. 226. New facilities.

Sec. 227. Alterations of existing facilities.

Sec. 228. Public transportation programs and activities in existing facilities and one car per train rule.

Sec. 229. Regulations.

Sec. 230. Interim accessibility requirements.

Sec. 231. Effective date.

Part II—Public Transportation by Intercity and Commuter Rail

Sec. 241. Definitions.

Sec. 242. Intercity and commuter rail actions considered discriminatory.

Sec. 243. Conformance of accessibility standards.

Sec. 244. Regulations.

Sec. 245. Interim accessibility requirements.

Sec. 246. Effective date.

Title III—Public Accommodations and Services Operated by Private Entities

Sec. 301. Definitions.

Sec. 302. Prohibition of discrimination by public accommodations.

Sec. 303. New construction and alterations in public accommodations and commercial facilities.

Sec. 304. Prohibition of discrimination in specified public transportation services provided by private entities.

Sec. 305. Study.

Sec. 306. Regulations.

Sec. 307. Exemptions for private clubs and religious organizations.

Sec. 308. Enforcement.

Sec. 309. Examinations and courses.

Sec. 310. Effective date.

Title IV—Telecommunications

Sec. 401. Telecommunication relay services for hearing-impaired and speech-impaired individuals.

Sec. 402. Closed-captioning of public service announcements.

Title V—Miscellaneous Provisions

Sec. 501. Construction.

Sec. 502. State immunity.

Sec. 503. Prohibition against retaliation and coercion.

Sec. 504. Regulations by the Architectural and Transportation Barriers Compliance Board.

Sec. 505. Attorney's fees.

Sec. 506. Technical assistance.

Sec. 507. Federal wilderness areas.

Sec. 508. Transvestites.

Sec. 509. Coverage of Congressional and the agencies of the legislative branch.

Sec. 510. Illegal use of drugs.

Sec. 511. Definitions.

Sec. 512. Amendments to the Rehabilitation Act.

Sec. 513. Alternative means of dispute resolution.

Sec. 514. Severability.

Section 2. Findings and Purposes.

(a) Findings.—The Congress finds that—

(1) some 43,000,000 Americans have one or more physical or mental disabilities, and the number is increasing as the population as a whole is growing older;

(2) historically, society has tended to isolate and segregate individuals with disabilities, and, despite some improvements, such forms of discrimination against individuals with disabilities continue to be a serious and pervasive social problem;

(3) discrimination against individuals with disabilities persists in such critical areas as employment, housing, public accommodations, education, transportation, communication, recreation, institutionalization, health services, voting, and access to public services;

(4) unlike individuals who have experienced discrimination on the basis of race, color, sex, national origin, religion, or age, individuals who have experienced discrimination on the basis of disability have often had no legal recourse to redress such discrimination;

(5) individuals with disabilities continually encounter various forms of discrimination, including outright intentional exclusion, the discriminatory effects of architectural, transportation, and communication barriers, overprotective rules

and policies, failure to make modifications to existing facilities and practices, exclusionary qualification standards and criteria, segregation, and relegation to lesser services, programs, activities, benefits, jobs, or other opportunities;

(6) census data, national polls, and other studies have documented that people with disabilities, as a group, occupy an inferior status in our society, and are severely disadvantaged socially, vocationally, economically, and educationally;

(7) individuals with disabilities are a discrete and insular minority who have been faced with restrictions and limitations, subjected to a history of purposeful unequal treatment, and relegated to a position of political powerlessness in our society, based on characteristics that are beyond the control of such individuals and resulting from stereotypic assumptions not truly indicative of the individual ability of such individuals to participate in, and contribute to, society;

(8) the Nation's proper goals regarding individuals with disabilities are to assure equality of opportunity, full participation, independent living, and economic self-sufficiency for such individuals; and

(9) the continuing existence of unfair and unnecessary discrimination and prejudice denies people with disabilities the opportunity to compete on an equal basis and to pursue those opportunities for which our free society is justifiably famous, and costs the United States billions of dollars in unnecessary expenses resulting from dependency and nonproductivity.

(b) Purpose.—It is the purpose of this Act—

(1) to provide a clear and comprehensive national mandate for the elimination of discrimination against individuals with disabilities;

(2) to provide clear, strong, consistent, enforceable standards addressing discrimination against individuals with disabilities;

(3) to ensure that the Federal Government plays a central role in enforcing the standards established in this Act on behalf of individuals with disabilities; and

(4) to invoke the sweep of congressional authority, including the power to enforce the fourteenth amendment and to regulate commerce, in order to address the major areas of discrimination faced day-to-day by people with disabilities.

Section 3. Definitions.

As used in this Act:

(1) Auxiliary aids and services.—The term "auxiliary aids and services" includes—

(A) qualified interpreters or other effective methods of making aurally delivered materials available to individuals with hearing impairments;

(B) qualified readers, taped texts, or other effective methods of making visually delivered materials available to individuals with visual impairments;

(C) acquisition or modification of equipment or devices; and

(D) other similar services and actions.

(2) Disability.—The term "disability" means, with respect to an individual—

(A) a physical or mental impairment that substantially limits one or more of the major life activities of such individual;

(B) a record of such an impairment; or

(C) being regarded as having such an impairment.

(3) State.—The term "State" means each of the several States, the District of Columbia, the Commonwealth of Puerto Rico, Guam, American Samoa, the Virgin Islands, the Trust Territory of the Pacific Islands, and the Commonwealth of the Northern Mariana Islands.

Title I—Employment

Section 101. Definitions

As used in this title:

(1) Commission.—The term "Commission" means the Equal Employment

Opportunity Commission established by section 705 of the Civil Rights Act of 1964 (42 U.S.C. 2000e-4).

(2) Covered entity.—The term "covered entity" means an employer, employment agency, labor organization, or joint labor-management committee.

(3) Direct threat.—The term "direct threat" means a significant risk to the health or safety of others that cannot be eliminated by reasonable accommodation.

(4) Employee.—The term "employee" means an individual employed by an employer.

(5) Employer.—

(A) In general.—The term "employer" means a person engaged in an industry affecting commerce who has 15 or more employees for each working day in each of 20 or more calendar weeks in the current or preceding calendar year, and any agent of such person, except that, for two years following the effective date of this title, an employer means a person engaged in an industry affecting commerce who has 25 or more employees for each working day in each of 20 or more calendar weeks in the current or preceding year, and any agent of such person.

(B) Exceptions.—The term "employer" does not include—

(i) the United States, a corporation wholly owned by the government of the United States, or an Indian tribe; or

(ii) a bona fide private membership club (other than a labor organization) that is exempt from taxation under section 501(c) of the Internal Revenue Code of 1986.

(6) Illegal use of drugs.—

(A) In general.—The term "illegal use of drugs" means the use of drugs, the possession or distribution of which is unlawful under the Controlled Substances Act (21 U.S.C. 812). Such term does not include the use of a drug taken under supervision by a licensed health care professional, or other uses authorized by the Controlled Substances Act or other provisions of Federal law.

(B) Drugs.—The term "drug" means a controlled substance, as defined in schedules I through V of section 202 of the Controlled Substances Act.

(7) Person etc.—The terms "person", "labor organization", "employment agency", "commerce", and "industry affecting commerce", shall have the same meaning given such terms in section 701 of the Civil Rights Act of 1964 (42 U.S.C. 2000e).

(8) Qualified individual with a disability.—The term "qualified individual with a disability" means an individual with a disability who, with or without reasonable accommodation, can perform the essential functions of the employment position that such individual holds or desires. For the purposes of this title, consideration shall be given to the employer's judgment as to what functions of a job are essential, and if an employer has prepared a written description before advertising or interviewing applicants for the job, this description shall be considered evidence of the essential functions of the job.

(9) Reasonable accommodation. — The term "reasonable accommodation" may include—

(A) making existing facilities used by employees readily accessible to and usable by individuals with disabilities; and

(B) job restructuring, part-time or modified work schedules, reassignment to a vacant position, acquisition or modification of equipment or devices, appropriate adjustment or modifications of examinations, training materials or policies, the provision of qualified readers or interpreters, and other similar accommodations for individuals with disabilities.

(10) Undue hardship.—

(A) In general.—The term "undue hardship" means an action requiring significant difficulty or expense, when considered in light of the factors set forth in subparagraph (B).

(B) Factors to be considered.—In determining whether an accommodation would impose an undue hardship on a covered entity, factors to be considered include—

(i) the nature and cost of the accommodation needed under this Act;

(ii) the overall financial resources of the facility or facilities involved in the provision of the reasonable accommodation; the number of persons employed at such facility; the effect on expenses and resources, or the impact otherwise of such accommodation upon the operation of the facility;

(iii) the overall financial resources of the covered entity; the overall size of the business of a covered entity with respect to the number of its employees; the number, type, and location of its facilities; and

(iv) the type of operation or operations of the covered entity, including the composition, structure, and functions of the workforce of such entity; the geographic separateness, administrative, or fiscal relationship of the facility or facilities in question to the covered entity.

Section 102. Discrimination.

(a) General rule.—No covered entity shall discriminate against a qualified individual with a disability because of the disability of such individual in regard to job application procedures, the hiring, advancement, or discharge of employees, employee compensation, job training, and other terms, conditions, and privileges of employment.

(b) Construction.—As used in subsection (a), the term "discriminate" includes—

(1) limiting, segregating, or classifying a job applicant or employee in a way that adversely affects the opportunities or status of such applicant or employee because of the disability of such applicant or employee;

(2) participating in a contractual or other arrangement or relationship that has the effect of subjecting a covered entity's qualified applicant or employee with a disability to the discrimination prohibited by this title (such relationship includes a relationship with an employment or referral agency, labor union, an organization providing fringe benefits to an employee of the covered entity, or an organization providing training and apprenticeship programs);

(3) utilizing standards, criteria, or methods of administration—

(A) that have the effect of discrimination on the basis of disability; or

(B) that perpetuate the discrimination of others who are subject to common administrative control;

(4) excluding or otherwise denying equal jobs or benefits to a qualified individual because of the known disability of an individual with whom the qualified individual is known to have a relationship or association;

(5)(A) not making reasonable accommodations to the known physical or mental limitations of an otherwise qualified individual with a disability who is an applicant or employee, unless such covered entity can demonstrate that the accommodation would impose an undue hardship on the operation of the business of such covered entity; or

(B) denying employment opportunities to a job applicant or employee who is an otherwise qualified individual with a disability, if such denial is based on the need of such covered entity to make reasonable accommodation to the physical or mental impairments of the employee or applicant;

(6) using qualification standards, employment tests or other selection criteria that screen out or tend to screen out an individual with a disability or a class of individuals with disabilities unless the standard, test or other selection criteria, as used by the covered entity, is shown to be job-related for the position in question and is consistent with business necessity; and

(7) failing to select and administer tests concerning employment in the most effective manner to ensure that, when such test is administered to a job applicant or employee who has a disability that impairs sensory, manual, or speaking skills, such test results accurately reflect the skills, aptitude, or whatever other factor of such applicant or employee that such test purports to measure, rather than reflecting the impaired sensory, manual, or speaking skills of such employee or applicant (except where such skills are the factors that the test purports to measure).

(c) Medical examinations and inquiries.—

(1) In general.—The prohibition against discrimination as referred to in subsection (a) shall include medical examinations and inquiries.

(2) Preemployment.—

(A) Prohibited examination or inquiry.—Except as provided in paragraph (3), a covered entity shall not conduct a medical examination or make inquiries of a job applicant as to whether such applicant is an individual with a disability or as to the nature or severity of such disability.

(B) Acceptable inquiry.—A covered entity may make preemployment inquiries into the ability of an applicant to perform job-related functions.

(3) Employment entrance examination.—A covered entity may require a medical examination after an offer of employment has been made to a job applicant and prior to the commencement of the employment duties of such applicant, and may condition an offer of employment on the results of such examination, if—

(A) all entering employees are subjected to such an examination regardless of disability;

(B) information obtained regarding the medical condition or history of the applicant is collected and maintained on separate forms and in separate medical files and is treated as a confidential medical record, except that—

(i) supervisors and managers may be informed regarding necessary restrictions on the work or duties of the employee and necessary accommodations;

(ii) first aid and safety personnel may be informed, when appropriate, if the disability might require emergency treatment; and

(iii) government officials investigating compliance with this Act shall be provided relevant information on request; and

(C) the results of such examination are used only in accordance with this title.

(4) Examination and inquiry.—

(A) Prohibited examinations and inquiries.—A covered entity shall not require a medical examination and shall not make inquiries of an employee as to whether such employee is an individual with a disability or as to the nature or severity of the disability, unless such examination or inquiry is shown to be job-related and consistent with business necessity.

(B) Acceptable examinations and inquiries.—A covered entity may conduct voluntary medical examinations, including voluntary medical histories, which are part of an employee health program available to employees at that work site. A covered entity may make inquiries into the ability of an employee to perform job-related functions.

(C) Requirement. — Information obtained under subparagraph (B) regarding the medical condition or history of any employee are subject to the requirements of subparagraphs (B) and (C) of paragraph (3).

Section 103. Defenses.

(a) In general.—It may be a defense to a charge of discrimination under this Act that an alleged application of qualification standards, tests, or selection criteria that screen out or tend to screen out or otherwise deny a job or benefit to an individual with a disability has been shown to be job-related and consistent with business necessity, and such performance cannot be accomplished by reasonable accommodation, as required under this title.

(b) Qualification standards.—The term "qualification standards" may include a requirement that an individual shall not pose a direct threat to the health or safety of other individuals in the workplace.

(c) Religious entities.—

(1) In general.—This title shall not prohibit a religious corporation, association, educational institution, or society from giving preference in employment to individuals of a particular religion to perform work connected with the carrying on by such corporation, association, educational institution, or society of its activities.

(2) Religious tenets requirement.—Under this title, a religious organization may require that all applicants and employees conform to the religious tenets of such organization.

(d) List of infectious and communicable diseases.—

(1) In general.—The Secretary of Health and Human Services, not later than 6 months after the date of enactment of this Act, shall—

(A) review all infectious and communicable diseases which may be transmitted through handling the food supply;

(B) publish a list of infectious and communicable diseases which are transmitted through handling the food supply;

(C) publish the methods by which such diseases are transmitted; and

(D) widely disseminate such information regarding the list of diseases and their modes of transmissability to the general public.

Such list shall be updated annually.

(2) Applications.—In any case in which an individual has an infectious or communicable disease that is transmitted to others through the handling of food, that is included on the list developed by the Secretary of Health and Human Services under paragraph (1), and which cannot be eliminated by reasonable accommodation, a covered entity may refuse to assign or continue to assign such individual to a job involving food handling.

(3) Construction.—Nothing in this Act shall be construed to preempt, modify, or amend any State, county, or local law, ordinance, or regulation applicable to food handling which is designed to protect the public health from individuals who pose a significant risk to the health or safety of others, which cannot be eliminated by reasonable accommodation, pursuant to the list of infectious or communicable diseases and the modes of transmissability published by the Secretary of Health and Human Services.

Section 104. Illegal use of drugs and alcohol.

(a) Qualified individual with a disability.—For purposes of this title, the term "qualified individual with a disability" shall not include any employee or applicant who is currently engaging in the illegal use of drugs, when the covered entity acts on the basis of such use.

(b) Rules of construction.—Nothing in subsection (a) shall be construed to exclude as a qualified individual with a disability an individual who—

(1) has successfully completed a supervised drug rehabilitation program and is no longer engaging in the illegal use of drugs, or has otherwise been rehabilitated successfully and is no longer engaging in such use;

(2) is participating in a supervised rehabilitation program and is no longer engaging in such use; or

(3) is erroneously regarded as engaging in such use, but is not engaging in such use; except that it shall not be a violation of this Act for a covered entity to adopt or administer reasonable policies or procedures, including but not limited to drug testing, designed to ensure that an individual described in paragraph (1) or (2) is no longer engaging in the illegal use of drugs.

(c) Authority of covered entity.—A covered entity—

(1) may prohibit the illegal use of drugs and the use [of] alcohol at the workplace by all employees;

(2) may require that employees shall not be under the influence of alcohol or be engaging in the illegal use of drugs at the workplace;

(3) may require that employees behave in conformance with the requirements established under the Drug-Free Workplace Act of 1988 (41 U.S.C. 701 et seq.);

(4) may hold an employee who engages in the illegal use of drugs or who is an alcoholic to the same qualification standards for employment or job performance and behavior that such entity holds other employees, even if any unsatisfactory performance or behavior is related to the drug use or alcoholism of such employee; and

(5) may, with respect to Federal regulations regarding alcohol and the illegal use of drugs, require that—

(A) employees comply with the standards established in such regulations of the Department of Defense, if the employees of the covered entity are employed in an industry subject to such regulations, including complying with regulations (if any) that apply to employment in sensitive positions in such an industry, in the case of employees of the covered entity who are employed in such positions (as defined in the regulations of the Department of Defense);

(B) employees comply with the standards established in such regulations of the Nuclear Regulatory Commission, if the employees of the covered entity are employed in an industry subject to such regulations, including complying with regulations (if any) that apply to employment in sensitive positions in such an industry, in the case of employees of the covered entity who are employed in such positions (as defined in the regulations of the Nuclear Regulatory Commission); and

(C) employees comply with the standards established in such regulations of the Department of Transportation, if the employees of the covered entity are employed in a transportation industry subject to such regulations, including complying with such regulations (if any) that apply to employment in sensitive positions in such an industry, in the case of employees of the covered entity who are employed in such positions (as defined in the regulations of the Department of Transportation).

(d) Drug testing.—

(1) In general.—For purposes of this title, a test to determine the illegal use of drugs shall not be considered a medical examination.

(2) Construction. — Nothing in this title shall be construed to encourage, prohibit, or authorize the conducting of drug testing for the illegal use of drugs by job applicants or employees or making employment decisions based on such test results.

(e) Transportation employees.— Nothing in this title shall be construed to encourage, prohibit, restrict, or authorize the otherwise lawful exercise by entities subject to the jurisdiction of the Department of Transportation of authority to—

(1) test employees of such entities in, and applicants for, positions involving safety-sensitive duties for the illegal use of drugs and for on-duty impairment by alcohol; and

(2) remove such persons who test positive for illegal use of drugs and on-duty impairment by alcohol pursuant to paragraph (1) from safety-sensitive duties in implementing subsection (c).

Section 105. Posting notices.

Every employer, employment agency, labor organization, or joint labor-management committee covered under this title shall post notices in an accessible format to applicants, employees, and members describing the applicable provisions of this Act, in the manner prescribed by section 711 of the Civil Rights Act of 1964 (42 U.S.C. 2000e-10).

Section 106. Regulations.

Not later than 1 year after the date of enactment of this Act, the Commission shall issue regulations in an accessible format to carry out this title in accordance with subchapter II of chapter 5 of title 5, United States Code.

Section 107. Enforcement.

(a) Powers, remedies, and procedures.—The powers, remedies, and procedures set forth in sections 705, 706, 707, 709, and 710 of the Civil Rights Act of 1964 (42 U.S.C. 2000e-4, 2000e-5, 2000e-6, 2000e-8, and 2000e-9) shall be the powers, remedies, and procedures this title provides to the Commission, to the Attorney General, or to any person alleging discrimination on the basis of disability in violation of any provision of this Act, or regulations promulgated under section 106, concerning employment.

(b) Coordination.—The agencies with enforcement authority for actions which allege employment discrimination under this title and under the Rehabilitation Act of 1973 shall develop procedures to ensure that administrative complaints filed under this title and under the Rehabilitation Act of 1973 are dealt with in a manner that avoids duplication of effort and prevents imposition of inconsistent or conflicting standards for the same requirements under this title and the Rehabilitation Act of 1973. The Commission, the Attorney General, and the Office of Federal Contract Compliance Programs shall establish such coordinating mechanisms (similar to provisions contained in the joint regulations promulgated by the Commission and the Attorney General at part 42 of title 28 and part 1691 of title 29, Code of Federal Regulations, and the Memorandum of Understanding between the Commission and the Office of Federal Contract Compliance Programs dated January 16, 1981 (46 Fed. Reg. 7435, January 23, 1981)) in regulations implementing this title and Rehabilitation Act of 1973 not later than 18 months after the date of enactment of this Act.

Section 108. Effective date.

This title shall become effective 24 months after the date of enactment.

Appendix

Suggested Solutions

Chapter One

Exercise 1.1

1. Sally is not a person with a disability. Temporary, nonchronic impairments with little or no long-term impact, such as a broken ankle, are not usually substantially limiting and therefore do not constitute a disability. The employer may decide to move her desk anyway.
2. Tom is a person with a disability who may need to be accommodated. Although a herniated disc may be temporary, it will likely be considered a disability due to its severity and long-term impact.
3. Mary is a person with a disability who may need to be accommodated. Although her diabetes may be presently under control, she still suffers from a physiological disorder. Diabetes is listed in the ADA as an example of a disability.
4. Harry is not a person with a disability. Homosexuality is a behavior that does not constitute a disability. It should be noted, however, that if an employer is not certain that an applicant is HIV positive but bases an employment decision on the belief that others will react negatively because of the perceived disability, the employer has violated the act. Moreover, in some states, Harry may have an independent basis for a suit based on harassment.
5. John is a person regarded as having an impairment. Someone with a physical deformity cannot be discriminated against because of an employer's fear that customers will react negatively to the person's appearance.

Exercise 1.2

1. Lena is a person with a record of impairment under the ADA. Under the ADA a person with a history of cancer has a record of disability. The act seeks to protect people like Lena from being discriminated against because of this medical history.
2. Nina is not a person with a record of impairment under the ADA. Although the injury is probably contained in a medical record, Nina is not protected by the ADA since her broken arm was a temporary condition with no negative, ongoing impact.
3. Michael is a person with a record of impairment under the ADA. While those currently using illegal drugs are not covered by the ADA, the act protects those, like Michael, who are not using drugs but are recovering from their addiction.
4. Charles is not a person with a record of impairment under the ADA. Charles is not protected by the ADA since advanced age is not an impairment. Various medical conditions that are associated with age such as arthritis and hearing loss, however, would be considered impairments. Charles would be covered by the federal Age Discrimination in Employment Act and possibly by state law.

Exercise 1.3

1. Ron is an individual regarded as having an impairment. The ADA protects those falsely believed to possess a substantially limiting impairment.
2. Martha is not an individual regarded as having an impairment because pregnancy is not considered a disability under the ADA. However, if a woman is denied an employment opportunity because she is perceived as being pregnant and more likely to become sick because of her pregnancy, then she could be protected by the ADA.
3. Rene is an individual regarded as having an impairment. A person who has had a mild heart attack and has recovered from it cannot be treated differently because of concerns about another heart attack.
4. Lisa is not an individual regarded as having a disability. Although regarded as difficult to work with, her quick temper does not qualify as a perceived disability substantially limiting one or more major life activities.

Chapter Two

Exercise 2.1

1. By telling the employment agency to look for only healthy applicants, the human resources manager has violated the ADA. Qualification standards or selection criteria that screen out an individual with a disability must be job related and consistent with business necessity. A person's healthy appearance is clearly not job related. It makes no difference that the agency, rather than the human resources manager, asks the unlawful question. Both would be liable for violating the ADA.
2. By removing Angela from consideration due to her mother's disability, Angela's employer violated the ADA. Under the ADA, an employer cannot deny a promotion to a qualified individual based on a relationship or association with a person with a disability.
3. Laura's decision to deny Henry the opportunity to attend the computer training course violated the ADA. Under the ADA, people like Henry who have been treated for a disability cannot be treated differently by an employer due to a record of impairment.
4. Whether the manager's decision to discharge John violates the ADA depends on whether keeping the job open constitutes an undue hardship. If John was in a specialized position, like executive chef at a four-star restaurant, it might be an undue hardship. If John cannot perform the essential functions of the job with or without reasonable accommodation, he may be terminated.
5. By refusing to hire Alice due to her cosmetic disfigurement, a condition that constitutes a disability under the ADA, the employer violated the ADA.

Exercise 2.2

1. Carol Ann should meet with Ray and discuss his performance problems in the same way that she would with any other employee. Employers can and should hold

employees with disabilities to the same standards as all other employees. In addition, Carol Ann may be able to find a reasonable accommodation to assist Ray.

2. Joe should have offered Michael the opportunity to work overtime. An employer should not give employees with disabilities special treatment. It is not Joe's role to decide if Michael's health imposes limitations.

3. Kevin should not have transferred Larry to another department. The ADA prohibits employers from segregating employees because of a disability. If Kevin felt that Larry was not performing well due to hearing problems, he should have required medical or other professional inquiries that are consistent with business necessity and that are job related to discover whether the poor performance was disability related and whether it required reasonable accommodation.

Chapter Three

Exercise 3.1

1. Carrying boxes probably is not an essential function of an accounting clerk's position. If the function was removed from the job, the basic purpose of the accounting clerk position would still be intact.
2. Lifting unconscious adults probably is an essential function of a ward nurse's job. Even if a task is rarely performed, removing it from a position might have dire consequences. The result is that this is an essential function.
3. The ability to deliver medical equipment probably would be an essential function only if the salesperson regularly delivered the goods and there were no other employees available to do it.
4. Being able to prepare meals is an essential function of a short-order cook. It is the reason the position exists.
5. The ability to type probably would not be an essential function of a claims adjuster's position. It seems likely that there would be other insurance company employees available to type reports.

Exercise 3.2

Essential functions and responsibilities

1. Inputs letters, memoranda, mailing lists, and other documents on a word processor or typewriter.
2. Answers telephone calls and records messages.
3. Transcribes dictation.
4. Photocopies documents.
5. Files, retrieves, and organizes documents in file cabinets and storage areas.

Marginal functions

1. Occasionally uses company car for errands.
2. Delivers interoffice correspondence and messages.

Knowledge, ability, and other job requirements

1. Level of knowledge and skill equivalent to that ordinarily acquired through graduation from high school and secretarial training school.
2. Ability to input at least 65 words per minute.
3. Working proficiency in WordPerfect® or other word processing software programs.
4. A high degree of organizational ability.
5. Must adhere to company personnel policies and practices, including attendance from 9:00 A.M. to 5:00 P.M. from Monday through Friday of each week.

The above statements are intended to describe the general nature and level of the work being performed by people assigned this job. They are not exhaustive lists of all duties, responsibilities, knowledge, skills, and abilities associated with this job. The company reserves the right to alter or modify this job description, with or without notice.

Chapter Four

Exercise 4.1

1. No. The school system does not have to accommodate Larry. The ADA requires only that employers reasonably accommodate individuals with disabilities who are otherwise qualified. Larry is not otherwise qualified for the position because he lacks the requisite experience.
2. No. The hotel does not have to accommodate Peggy. Peggy can no longer perform the essential functions of the job even with a reasonable accommodation. Thus, Peggy is not protected by the ADA.
3. Yes. The company has an obligation to provide a sign language interpreter or some other reasonable accommodation to Melvin. Under the ADA, an employer must provide an employee with a disability with reasonable accommodation necessary to enable the employee to participate in the evaluation process.
4. No. The company does not have to accommodate Blaine. It has the right to request verification of his impairment and need not accommodate him if he cannot provide evidence of the disability.
5. No. The company does not have to accommodate Mavis. While she apparently would prefer to live in Miami, that relocation is not required for her disability since her physician has said she could return to work in Chicago.
6. Yes. The hospital probably should accommodate Jake. While it will be varying from its policies, the variation will enable Jake to perform his job. There is no hardship to the hospital because there are other X-ray technicians available to cover when Jake is on breaks.

Suggested Solutions

Chapter Five

Exercise 5.1

1. The firm probably will have to accommodate Alex. It is unlikely that it will be able to demonstrate that an annual expense of $900 to provide an interpreter constitutes an undue hardship.
2. The firm will have to accommodate Leslie if there is a position open. An employee's fear of working with a disabled employee is one of the barriers to employment that the ADA was designed to correct.
3. The firm probably has to accommodate Ken, since the loading may not be an essential function of the job. Although it requires some job restructuring, asking a full-time employee who works 40 hours a week to spend 3 hours per week on a different task is unlikely to cause an undue hardship.
4. The firm probably will have to accommodate Marilyn. The ADA requires that employers modify employment policies if necessary; this might be such a policy that would have to be modified to accommodate Marilyn.
5. The firm probably would not be required to accommodate Dennis. While there are many facts that would be considered, an employer may not be required to keep a facility heated and secure for an evening employee when it has never done so.

Chapter Six

Exercise 6.1

1. This is an inappropriate question. You may only inquire about the ability to perform specific job-related functions. However, you may state your attendance standards and ask the applicant if he or she will have any trouble adhering to them.
2. This is an appropriate question. This question is limited to inquiring about the applicant's ability to perform a specific, essential function of the job.
3. This is an inappropriate question. This is an example of fishing about an individual's physical condition that has nothing to do with the position for which application is made.
4. This is an appropriate question. This is another example of a question that is limited in scope to the applicant's ability to perform a specific job-related function.

5–8. These are all inappropriate questions. They do not address the applicant's ability to perform job-related functions.

Chapter Seven

Exercise 7.1

1. This is an appropriate employment practice. The ADA requires that, if an employer requires a medical examination for a particular class of employees, all employees entering that particular job classification or category must be subject to a medical examination regardless of actual or suspected disability. Thus, examinations may be required of all kitchen workers, even if not required for other employees.
2. This may be an appropriate employment practice. Information obtained during the medical examination must be kept confidential. Supervisors and managers may be informed only of accommodations and/or work restrictions if any are necessary. However, safety personnel or first-aid staff may be informed of medical information if it is necessary to enable them to assist in the event of an emergency. If Maria's supervisor is safety personnel who would need to know of the condition to assist in an emergency, it would be appropriate to inform him.
3. Lyle's advice is incorrect. The ADA does not prohibit the discharge of an employee for refusing to take a preemployment medical examination given to all employees.
4. This is an inappropriate employment practice. The employer may not withdraw a job offer because of concern that at some time in the future the employee will be unable to function due to an illness.
5. This probably is an appropriate employment practice. Using his arms is likely to be an essential function of the security guard's job. However, the medical examination should be limited to assessing the arm's mobility so that the employer can make a determination of Louis's fitness for duty.

Chapter Eight

Exercise 8.1

1. This violates the ADA. The employer can require only that the driver be able to perform certain functions, such as lifting patients or driving an ambulance.
2. This is acceptable under the ADA. However, the employer can find that an applicant poses a direct threat only where there is a significant risk of substantial harm, where that risk is not remote, where that risk is based on current medical knowledge or the best available objective evidence, and where that risk cannot be reasonably accommodated.
3. This could violate the ADA if the applicant has an eye condition that constitutes a disability and prevents her from having 20-20 vision. It is not a business necessity since an applicant with corrective lenses can drive a bus.
4. This complies with the ADA. The test is job related and a business necessity since the orderly will be performing this essential function.
5. This violates the ADA. There is no objective evidence of a threat of AIDS to co-workers.
6. This violates the ADA. He may not need to read music in order to have the performing skills required.

Suggested Solutions

Chapter Nine

Exercise 9.1

1. Jennifer will be considered disabled under the ADA. Even an individual who currently is using prescribed medication is an individual with a disability.
2. Reggie will not be considered disabled under the ADA. In order to be protected by the ADA, an individual must refrain from drug use *and* be receiving treatment or has been successfully rehabilitated. Since Reggie is currently using cocaine, he is not protected by the ADA.
3. Alex will be considered disabled under the ADA. Individuals who are not using illegal drugs but who are erroneously perceived as currently using illegal drugs are protected by the ADA.
4. Marsha will not be considered disabled under the ADA. A person currently using illegal drugs is not protected by the ADA, whether or not that person is enrolled in a rehabilitation program.
5. Glen will be considered disabled under the ADA even though the rehabilitation programs have not been successful.

Chapter Ten

Exercise 10.1

1. True. The EEOC enforces Title I of the ADA. A job applicant or employee who believes he or she has been discriminated against on the basis of disability in employment by a private, state, or local government employer, labor union, employment agency, or joint labor-management committee can file a charge with the EEOC.
2. False. An individual must file a charge with the EEOC before he or she can file a lawsuit. Upon filing a charge, the party must wait 180 days and then may request a right to sue letter from the EEOC. The charging party will then have 90 days to file suit after receiving the notice of the right to sue.
3. True. The relief or remedies available for employment discrimination may include hiring, reinstatement, promotion, back pay, front pay, reasonable accommodation, or other actions that will make an individual whole. Attorneys' fees, expert witness fees, court costs, and compensatory and punitive damages are also available.
4. True. Damages may be available to compensate for actual monetary losses, for future monetary losses, and for mental anguish and inconvenience.
5. False. The ADA requires that a charge be filed with the EEOC within 180 days or 300 days, if in a state that has a state agency that processes charges. Here, Louise did not file within either time period and, thus, her claim is time barred; that is, her charge will not be addressed. She has no remedies available to her under the ADA.

Glossary

direct threat A significant risk of substantial harm to the health or safety of the individual or others that cannot be eliminated or reduced by reasonable accommodation.

disability A physical or mental impairment that substantially limits one or more major life activities, a record of such impairment, or being regarded as having such impairment.

essential functions A job function may be essential for one of the following reasons: (1) the position exists to perform that function, (2) there are only a limited number of employees available to perform that function, and (3) the function is so specialized that the incumbent is hired for his or her expertise or ability to perform that function.

major life activities Functions such as caring for oneself, performing manual tasks, walking, seeing, hearing, speaking, breathing, learning, and working.

mental impairment Any mental or physiological disorder such as mental retardation, organic brain syndrome, emotional or mental illness, and specific learning disabilities.

physical impairment Any physiological disorder or condition or anatomical loss affecting one or more of the body's systems.

preemployment inquiries Questions asked of job applicants prior to a hiring decision. Under the ADA, these questions may relate only to the ability to perform specific job-related functions.

preemployment medical examinations Medical examinations that are required of job applicants prior to a final hiring decision. Under the ADA, they may be required only of applicants *after* a conditional offer of employment has been extended.

qualification standards The personal and professional attributes established by an employer that an individual must meet in order to be eligible for the position held or desired.

qualified individual with a disability An individual with a disability who (1) satisfies the requisite skill, experience, education, and other job-related requirements of a position; and (2) can perform the essential functions of the position, with or without reasonable accommodation.

reasonable accommodation A change in the work environment that enables an applicant or employee with a disability to participate in all of the benefits of the workplace.

record of impairment A job applicant's or employee's history of a physical or mental difficulty. Under the ADA, the person will be considered to have a disability if the person has a record of a physical or mental impairment that itself would qualify as a disability under the ADA or if the person has been misclassified as having such an impairment.

regarded as having an impairment Those without a disability but protected by the ADA because they are perceived as having a disability.

substantially limits With respect to a disability, anything that renders an individual (1) unable to perform a major life activity that the average person in the general population can perform or (2) significantly restricts him or her in the performance of a major life activity as compared to the average person in the general population.

undue hardship An action that is excessively costly, extensive, substantial, or disruptive, or that would fundamentally alter the nature or operation of the business.

THE BUSINESS SKILLS EXPRESS SERIES

This growing series of books addresses a broad range of key business skills and topics to meet the needs of employees, human resource departments, and training consultants.

To obtain information about these and other Business Skills Express books, please call Business One IRWIN toll free at: 1-800-634-3966.

Effective Performance Management	ISBN	1-55623-867-3
Hiring the Best	ISBN	1-55623-865-7
Writing that Works	ISBN	1-55623-856-8
Customer Service Excellence	ISBN	1-55623-969-6
Writing for Business Results	ISBN	1-55623-854-1
Powerful Presentation Skills	ISBN	1-55623-870-3
Meetings that Work	ISBN	1-55623-866-5
Effective Teamwork	ISBN	1-55623-880-0
Time Management	ISBN	1-55623-888-6
Assertiveness Skills	ISBN	1-55623-857-6
Motivation at Work	ISBN	1-55623-868-1
Overcoming Anxiety at Work	ISBN	1-55623-869-X
Positive Politics at Work	ISBN	1-55623-879-7
Telephone Skills at Work	ISBN	1-55623-858-4
Managing Conflict at Work	ISBN	1-55623-890-8
The New Supervisor: Skills for Success	ISBN	1-55623-762-6
The *Americans with Disabilities Act*: What Supervisors Need to Know	ISBN	1-55623-889-4